ABOVE: Locomotive change at Carlisle Citadel, 2014 style: While locomotive changes at the border city were a regular feature in steam days, an LMS Duchess Pacific would normally hand over to another locomotive of the same class. However, on September 27, LNER A4 Pacific No. 60009 *Union of South Africa,* **which had worked the Railway Touring Company's 'Scottish Lowlander' from Carstairs, is replaced by No. 46233** *Duchess of Sutherland* **which will take the train over Shap to Carnforth.** DAVE RODGERS

INTRODUCTION

O ne of the greatest celebrations ever held in the railway heritage sector began on July 3, 2013. Marking the 75th anniversary of Britain's 126mph world speed steam record set by LNER streamlined A4 Pacific No. 4468 *Mallard* on Stoke Bank in Lincolnshire. All six surviving class members, including two temporarily repatriated from North America, were brought together at the National Railway Museum in York for the first of three phenomenally successful Great Gatherings under the banner of Mallard 75.

Also in the summer of 2013, two other preservation icons marked their 75th birthdays – LMS Princess Coronation Pacifics No. 46233 *Duchess of Sutherland* and No. 6229 *Duchess of Hamilton.*

Both celebrations were extremely low-key affairs when compared with Mallard 75.

It is said that history does not remember the 'also rans': taking a footballing analogy, who recalls the team that finished runners-up in the Premier League or losing finalists in the FA Cup two or three seasons on?

When they reclaimed the world record from Nazi Germany, *Mallard* driver Joe Duddington and fireman Thomas Bray also snatched the British record back from their greatest rivals, the LMS.

Just over a year before, on June 29, 1937, equally daring Crewe North driver Tom Clark

had beaten the LNER by taking chief mechanical engineer William Stanier's new Princess Coronation streamlined Pacific No. 6220 *Coronation* to a claimed 114mph.

In the Thirties, the zenith of the steam age, the LMS and LNER competed to see whose express trains could get from London to Scotland in the fastest time.

Mallard had the benefit of the LNER's great racetrack, Stoke Bank, while *Coronation* set its record on the less favourable Madeley Bank.

THE LMS PRINCESS CORONATION CLASS COMPRISED THE MOST POWERFUL STEAM LOCOMOTIVES EVER TO BE BUILT FOR USE ON THE BRITISH RAILWAY NETWORK

Railway speed record attempts have rarely, if ever, been made on a level playing surface, almost all of them were achieved on different gradients, with different loadings and variable circumstances on the day.

The LMS Princess Coronations, some of which were streamlined as a response to

Gre... stea... Brit...

In terms of absolute power, examples were recorded as producing 3300hp under test, making them far more powerful than the diesel engines that replaced them.

Many experts have expressed the view that a Princess Coronation, or Duchess, as the non- and destreamlined versions were later known, could have easily given *Mallard* a run for its money if it had been allowed to stage a record attempt on Stoke Bank. Railway historians have long debated the comparative merits of both rival types.

Yet it is *Mallard* that holds the record, which given the modern-day speed restrictions on steam locomotives, will almost certainly never be broken.

Had the Second World War not brought the curtain down on the last great age of racing steam trains, it is almost certain that the LNER or LMS would have aimed to break the record once more.

So, rightly or wrongly, the Princess Coronation class must remain as the runner-up, the losing cup finalist beaten by a single goal.

That is sad, because there are many experts who claim that the Princess Coronations were the finest British express passenger locomotives ever built.

COVER: Top: the restreamlined No. 6229 *Duchess of Hamilton* **outside the Locomotion museum at Shildon.** LOCOMOTION
Bottom left: No. 46233 *Duchess of Sutherland* **at York station on June 29, 2013.** ROBIN JONES
Bottom right: No. 46229 *Duchess of Hamilton* **leaves Skipton on May 1, 1980.** BRIAN SHARPE
BACK COVER: Darkness and light: The painting of LMS Duchess No. 46238 *City of Carlisle* **that won the picture of the year award at the Guild of Railway Artists' Railart 2014 exhibition. It was the 17th successive year that the artist, John Austin, has topped the poll.**

ABOVE: Restreamlined Princess Coronation Pacific No. 6229 *Duchess of Hamilton* alongside its greatest rival, world record holding A4 No. 4468 *Mallard*, in the Great Hall at the National Railway Museum in York in February 2010. BRIAN SHARPE

New out of the box and all set to take Shap and Beattock by storm and then the world: No. 6220 *Coronation* pictured on May 25, 1937.

SO WHY DUCHESS 75 NOW?

It was in 1939 that a member of the class embarked on a visit to New York's World's Fair, an event of seismic headline-grabbing proportions designed to showcase the future world in an age of technology.

There, 'No. 6220 *Coronation*' was displayed among some of the world's finest new locomotive designs, which, as history records, were not the future of transport technology, but in many way the last blast of steam locomotive development before diesels and electric traction became standard. Nonetheless, at the fair, British technology was there with the very best, together with a complete LMS 'Coronation Scot' luxury named train.

However, all was not what it seemed to the millions of people who saw the Stanier masterpiece stateside.

The locomotive was an impostor, for the real No. 6220 *Coronation* was not painted in crimson lake livery, but in Caledonian Railway blue – and at the same time as crowds flocked to the fair to marvel at the latest inventions such as television sets, it was plying its trade over the West Coast Main Line between Euston and Glasgow.

What was on view was sister No. 6229

Author:
Robin Jones

Designer:
Leanne Lawrence

Reprographics:
Simon Duncan

Senior sub-editor:
Dan Sharp

Production manager:
Craig Lamb

Marketing manager:
Charlotte Park

Publisher:
Tim Hartley

Commercial director:
Nigel Hole

Publishing director:
Dan Savage

Published by:
Mortons Media Group Ltd,
Media Centre,
Morton Way, Horncastle,
Lincolnshire LN9 6JR
Tel: 01507 529529

Printed by:
William Gibbons and Sons,
Wolverhampton

ISBN:
978-1-909128-51-4

© Mortons Media Group Ltd.
All rights reserved. No part of this publication may be produced or transmitted in any form or by any means, electronic or mechanical, including photocopying, recording, or any information storage retrieval system without prior permission in writing from the publisher.

Credits:
All pictures marked * are published under a Creative Commons licence. Full details may be obtained at http://creativecommons.org/licences

www.classicmagazines.co.uk

The great adventure begins: the first of Stanier's streamlined Princess Coronation Pacifics No. 6220 *Coronation* is shunted by LNWR 'Cauliflower' 0-6-0 No. 8442 into platform 6 at Euston ahead of the press review trip on June 29, 1937, when the locomotive set a new British speed record of 114mph. The class name celebrated the coronation of King George VI on May 12, 1937. NRM

Duchess of Hamilton in disguise.

The outbreak of war did more than bring the last great decade of world steam to a swift and sudden end. It left No. 6229 *Duchess of Hamilton* marooned in the US.

Eventually, because of the desperate need for locomotives, it was brought back in 1942. Railway bosses were prepared to run the gauntlet of the German U-boat campaign against the Atlantic convoys.

Its luxury train did not return until 1946, but its articulated carriages would never again form part of the 'Coronation Scot'.

The end of the war also marked the demise of the LMS streamliners, for they had their air-smoothed casings removed, and took on the appearance of traditional steam locomotives.

The glitz and glamour may therefore have been stripped away, but the class entered a new world of legend. The non-streamlined Duchesses built up a huge following among the enthusiast fraternity for their displays of raw power. Many West Coast services in the Fifties produced 14, 15, and 16 coach loads, and often 17 on southbound services.

There was nothing that the Duchesses could not handle. It was not diesels that killed off the Duchesses, but the electrification of the West Coast route.

The last examples to be withdrawn were taken out of service 50 years ago, in the infamous cull of September 1964.

Sadly, the preservation movement had not evolved to the point where nascent heritage lines could have bought them straight out of service, and so their final journeys were made to the scrapyard – in all but three cases.

Thanks to the efforts of holiday camp supremo Billy Butlin, *Duchess of Hamilton*, the star of that US tour 75 years ago, survived against the odds to tell many more illustrious tales – and to regain its streamlined casing to become a flagship exhibit at the National

Rare window on the early Princess Coronations: this Dufaycolour transparency from the dawn of commercially available colour slide film was rediscovered by Gordon Hall among a collection of family photographs. Like most Dufaycolour images it is quite dense but the colours are true and although the train is travelling at some speed, judging by the exhaust, the whole image is remarkably sharp, despite being rated at just 2ASA! The slide had no details, but Gordon and friends worked out that it is the northbound 'Coronation Scot' emerging from under the bridge at Kingmoor near Carlisle, where the Waverley Route crossed the West Coast Main Line, maybe in late summer 1938/39? The locomotive may be No. 6222 *Queen Mary*. GORDON HALL COLLECTION

Railway Museum. It handed over the main line mantle to another ex-Butlins' locomotive, No. 6233 *Duchess of Sutherland*, to fly the flag for this stupendous class on the national network today.

Celebrating the anniversary of that epic journey in disguise to the States in 1939, here is

the story of one of the greatest of all steam locomotive types ever built, which may have missed out on a world record through fate and political circumstance.

Robin Jones
November 2014

CONTENTS

Representing the Princess Coronation Pacifics in their final form and livery, British Railways' Brunswick green, is No. 46233 *Duchess of Sutherland*, **seen heading past Ais Gill on May 22, 2013 with the Railway Touring Company's 'Cumbrian Mountain Express'.**
JOHN TITLOW

CHAPTER ONE

THE ROUTE OF THE DUCHESSES

LNWR Improved Precedent 2-4-0 No. 1532 *Hampden*. Designed by the 'King of Crewe' Francis Webb, a total of 168 were built in batches at the Crewe Works between 1887-1901. TONY HISGETT COLLECTION*

The true origins of both the Princess Coronation Pacifics and their streamlined rivals the A4s date back to the dawn of the British railway network, and in particular the rivalry between the two great routes that linked London to Scotland, and spanned many generations of railwaymen.

Neither the East Coast nor the West Coast Main Line was designed or built as a trunk route, nor even a single entity. Both came about as amalgamations of different companies' lines between the 1830s and the 1880s.

The seeds of the West Coast Main Line were sown in the wake of the phenomenal success of the opening of the world's first inter-city line, the Liverpool & Manchester Railway, in 1830.

Once it had become accepted and established, speculators looked to the building of more inter-city lines.

The first section of what is now the West Coast Main Line was the Grand Junction Railway linking Liverpool and Manchester to Birmingham via Crewe, Stafford, Wolverhampton and Perry Barr.

It opened in 1837, the year the London & Birmingham Railway was completed, linking Britain's two biggest cities via Coventry, Rugby and the Watford Gap. The pair shared a common terminus at Curzon Street station in Birmingham. Although passengers had to change trains, it was from then possible to travel all the way from London to Liverpool and Manchester by rail.

The Trent Valley Railway was opened in 1847 to give a more direct route from London to the North West, bypassing the existing route via Birmingham built by these two companies a decade before.

The Manchester & Birmingham Railway between Manchester and Crewe opened in stages between 1840 and 1846.

In 1846, all of these companies merged into one, the London & North Western Railway. Another section was the North Staffordshire Railway which in 1848 opened a route from Macclesfield, where it linked to the LNWR from Manchester) to Stafford and Colwich via

LMS Jubilee 4-6-0 No. 45699 *Galatea* hauls 'The Fellsman' across the stupendous Ribblehead Viaduct on the Settle to Carlisle line on July 2, 2014. Often named at the most beautiful route in Britain, the Settle and Carlisle came into existence following a petty disagreement between the LNWR and Midland Railway over access to the main west coast route. ANDREW/CC*

Stoke-on-Trent. However, because of squabbling between the two companies, through trains did not run until 1867.

Going northwards, the next link in the chain was the North Union Railway between Wigan and Preston. The first-ever railway merger, between the Wigan Branch Railway and the Wigan and Preston Junction Railway was authorised by an Act of Parliament in 1834.

In 1846, it was leased jointly by the Grand Junction Railway and the Manchester & Leeds Railway, becoming the Lancashire & Yorkshire Railway respectively. The LNWR owned around two thirds of the North Union and the L&Y around a third.

From July 26, 1889, the LNWR took control of the Parkside to Euxton section, although the line remained jointly owned until the Grouping of 1923. Eventually, the Lancaster & Carlisle Railway leased it from August 1, 1849, and amalgamated with it a decade later.

THE CONQUEST OF SHAP

The Lancaster & Carlisle was authorised on June 6, 1844, to, as its name suggests, build a line linking both cities. However, therein lay the problem.

The Westmorland Fells was the biggest obstacle between the two cities. The railway's directors looked at taking a route through Kendal and along Longsleddale, with a two

ABOVE: LNWR Improved Precedent No. 790 *Hardwicke*, the true star of the 1895 Race to the North, stands outside the Locomotion museum at Shildon in July 2014. It was preserved following withdrawal in 1932. To its right is LNWR 2-2-2 No. 3020 *Cornwall*, designed by locomotive superintendent Francis Trevithick and named after his home county. Addressing the desire for greater speed, his design featured a shorter wheelbase, positioning the boiler behind the driving axle. *Cornwall* was an exhibition at the Great Exhibition of 1851 at the Crystal Palace and is now part of the National Collection. LOCOMOTION

The competition: the Great Northern Railway class Stirling single No. 1 was designed by Patrick Stirling for express passenger work, hauling up to 26 passenger carriages at an average speed of 47mph. Their distinctive feature is a single pair of 8ft driving wheels. The sole-surviving example of a class of 53 built at Doncaster Works, No. 1, is now in the National Collection and is seen outside the Locomotion museum in May 2014, when it was paired again with an original GNR tender which had just been restored. RICHARD PEARSON/LOCOMOTION

mile tunnel under the Gatescarth Pass into Mardale and then on towards Bampton.

Other options included a railway over a barrage across Morecambe Bay and running round the Cumbrian coast.

Both routes would have bypassed Shap Fell. The gradient of the Longsleddale route would have been less than the 1-in-70 of the climb up and over Shap Fell, a route chosen by engineer Joseph Locke. The directors were concerned at the extra expense of using banking engines to push trains over the summit on this option.

A parliamentary inquiry into the choices was held to settle the dispute between the various parties, and Locke's longer and steeper route through the Lune Gorge and over Shap Fell, which missed out Kendal, was chosen.

Shap Summit was the highest point of the planned 69-mile route, 914ft above sea level. It was there that the first sod was cut in July 1844. The name Shap would become legendary in railway circles, for the awesome amount of power needed by locomotives to haul trains over the summit.

Great Northern Railway Stirling single 4-2-2 No. 544 with a rake of six-wheeled coaches.

It was originally intended to build a single-track line, but in January the following year it was announced that the line would be double track.

The railway opened between Lancaster to Oxenholme on September 22, 1846, the same day that services began running on a branch line from Oxenholme to Kendal opened. The Oxenholme to Carlisle section opened on December 17, 1846.

The project was the biggest single railway contract of the time and the contractor was

The classical station building in Birmingham's Curzon Street marked the meeting place of the first two major constituents of the West Coast Main Line, the Grand Junction and London & Birmingham railways. It has been earmarked for re-use as part of the proposed High Speed 2 Birmingham terminus. ROBIN JONES

Thomas Brassey in partnership with William Mackenzie and John Stephenson. At its height, 10,000 men were involved and the line was completed in 2½ years.

The cutting at Shap Summit was hacked through half a mile of rock, The gradient began 30 miles to the south at Carnforth, the final five miles being at 1-in-75, while to the north, the approach began at Carlisle, the last 10 miles being mostly 1-in-125.

The LNWR leased the L&CR in 1859, and took it over two decades later.

ACROSS THE BORDER

Beyond Carlisle, the Caledonian Railway completed the route into Scotland. The company was formed in the 1830s to link local railways around Glasgow and Edinburgh, and aimed to build the only cross-border main line at a time when it was thought only one was needed.

Empowered by the Caledonian Railway Act of 1845, the first section of its main line, between Carlisle and Beattock was opened on September 10, 1847.

At 1033ft above sea level, Beattock Summit is the highest point on the WCML in Scotland. Locomotives frequently required banking assistance in getting their heavy trains up the incline, particularly in the northbound direction, which had steeper gradients. There was an engine shed at Beattock with banking

locomotives on standby 24 hours a day to minimise train delays.

The line was completed to Glasgow and Edinburgh on February 15, 1848. The route to Glasgow used the earlier Glasgow, Garnkirk & Coatbridge, and the Wishaw & Coltness railways, which the Caledonian bought in 1846 and 1849 respectively.

From then, it was possible to travel between the two capitals. The route to Scotland was marketed by the LNWR as the Premier Line, and through trains comprised jointly owned West Coast Joint Stock carriages. The first direct London to Glasgow trains in the 1850s took 12½ hours to complete the 400-mile journey.

A new branch to Liverpool, bypassing the earlier Liverpool and Manchester line was opened in 1869, from Weaver Junction north of Crewe to Ditton Junction. In 1881, Northampton was connected to the trunk route when a loop was opened, following the quadrupling of the line from Euston to Rugby to boost capacity.

TWO RIVALS EMERGE

However, the Caledonian's wish to have the only cross-border route was doomed to fail.

It comes as a surprise to many to learn that the rival East Coast route was not begun in London, but at the Scottish end.

The North British Railway opened its line from Edinburgh to Berwick-on-Tweed in 1846. Four years later, the North Eastern Railway began running from Berwick-on-Tweed to Shaftholme, a small hamlet two miles north of Doncaster. There, it linked up with the Great Northern Railway, whose line from Shaftholme

to King's Cross, completed in 1850. The through route was opened on October 14, 1852, with the extension of GNR services into the new King's Cross station.

Each of the three companies built their lines to serve their local area, but in the background was the ultimate aim to link up to provide a trunk route from Edinburgh to London.

Elsewhere, in 1844 the Midland Counties Railway, the North Midland Railway and the Birmingham & Derby Junction Railway amalgamated into the Midland Railway, which emerged as another major rival to the LNWR for Anglo-Scottish traffic.

In the late 1860s a dispute arose between the two companies concerning access rights to the LNWR route to Scotland, initially over the shared use of Ingleton station. This led to the Midland building the Settle and Carlisle line – the highest main line in England and said by many to be the most beautiful – to link directly to the still-independent Caledonian Railway and gain its own route to Scotland.

Furthermore, the Glasgow & South Western and the North British railways had, by then, reached Carlisle, and saw the new Midland line as a means of challenging the Caledonian's monopoly on West Coast traffic to Glasgow and Edinburgh. Backed into a corner, the Midland built the Settle to Carlisle line and opened it in 1876.

At first, the competition between the routes was for volume of traffic, not speed. However, it became inevitable that sooner or later, there would be rivalry over which route could offer the complete journey from Scotland to London in the shortest time.

London's lost gateway to Scotland: the Euston Arch, built in 1837, and pictured in the Thirties, was the original entrance to Euston station. It was controversially demolished in 1961-62 when the station was rebuilt in the 1960s, with much of the original stone was relocated decades later. In March 2014 it was announced that a revived £1.2 billion scheme to rebuild London's Euston station for the High Speed 2 route to Birmingham and the North might include the reconstruction of the Doric arch. LMS/ROBIN JONES COLLECTION.

Midland Railway Kirtley 156 class 2-4-0 No. 158A was built in 1866 to a Matthew Kirtley design for express passenger workings to King's Cross, which was then the company's London terminus. The Midland Railway was derided for its small-engines policy, which saw very attractive, polished and superbly presented crimson-lake liveried but small locomotives used on its major routes, often having to double head or rely on banking engines because their individual power was insufficient.
No. 158A was rebuilt several times until it was finally withdrawn in 1947 after 81 years service at Nottingham, where it was being used as station pilot. It appeared at the Stephenson Centenary Celebrations in Chesterfield in 1948 and was then preserved at Derby Locomotive Works until moving to the Midland Railway-Butterley in 1975. Part of the National Collection, it is seen on display in the Matthew Kirtley Exhibition Hall at Swanwick Junction. ROBIN JONES

LMS Royal Scot 4-6-0 No. 46115 *Scots Guardsman* tackles Shap on March 1, 2014, with the Railway Touring Company's 'Winter Cumbrian Mountain Express'. The 1927-built locomotive was the star of the classic 1936 documentary film Night Mail about a LMS mail train from London to Scotland, and produced by the GPO Film Unit. WH Auden wrote a poem for the film, which included music by Benjamin Britten. NEIL SCOTT*

THE RACES TO THE NORTH

The east coast day express from King's Cross to Edinburgh became an hour quicker than its LNWR rival in 1862, but that company failed to rise to the challenge, and did not alter the west coast timing. By 1873, the Great Northern was running a more intensive service of express trains than either the LNWR or the Midland. Hauled by Patrick Stirling's single driving-wheel locomotives, GNR trains were some of the fastest in the world.

However, after the Settle and Carlisle route was opened, the Midland began to dominate the London-Glasgow traffic, running more daytime trains than the LNWR, and promoting the greater comfort of its coaches which, from 1874, included Pullman carriages imported from the USA.

However, the Settle & Carlisle never seriously competed with the West Coast Main Line in terms of speed, as opposed to comfort, because of its steeper gradients and greater length. Also, the Midland services that ran over it to Carlisle made more stops, to serve major cities in the Midlands and Yorkshire.

By late Victorian times, the public had long taken for granted the ability to travel quickly between long-distance destinations by rail,

and demanded faster journey times.

In late 1887, the east coast companies decided to allow third-class travel on their 'Flying Scotsman' express. On June 2 the following year, the LNWR and Caledonian responded by speeding up the 10am 'Scotch Express' so it could run from Euston to Edinburgh in nine hours, the same as the east coast alternative from King's Cross.

The east coast responded by increasing the speed of its services from July 1, 1888. There followed weeks of competition which historians later dubbed the first Race to the North.

While the west coast cut time off from its 10-hour journey time, the East Coast reduced its nine-hour journey by 30 minutes.

In retaliation, the west coast companies cut 30 minutes off, before the east coast again cut off half an hour. The west coast did likewise. The rivals were now running trains as fast as Victorian technology would permit.

On Bank Holiday Monday August 8, 1888, the west coast decided to match the east coast's eight-hour schedule, and maintained it for a week. The east coast partners then announced that from August 14, the journey would be cut to seven hours 45 minutes.

The day before, the west coast service ran from London to Edinburgh in seven hours 38 minutes, averaging 52.3mph.

The following day, the rivals reached agreement on minimum timings for their trains, and racing stopped.

While on August 31, a King's Cross-Edinburgh train hit an average speed of 52.7mph, already the rivals had reached agreement to end the races, with the east coast railways taking eight hours 15 minutes and the west coast eight hours and 30 minutes.

Seven years later, in the summer of 1895, however, the fierce rivalry erupted again, when the west coast partners saw that the completion of the Forth Bridge would provide their east coast counterparts with a shorter route to Dundee and Aberdeen.

The second Race to the North involved Kinnaber Junction, 38 miles south of Aberdeen, where the Caledonian and the North British routes merged before running into the Granite City over Caledonian metals as its finishing post.

Before the races, the timetabled service from King's Cross to Aberdeen took 12 hours 20 minutes. On August 20, the 523-mile east coast Aberdeen trip took eight hours 40 minutes, with an average speed of 60.4mph.

Two days later, the west coast fought back, when the Francis Webb's LNWR Improved Precedent express passenger 2-4-0 No. 790 *Hardwicke* took two hours and six minutes to cover the 141 miles from Crewe to Carlisle, reaching 88mph in places, with an average speed of 67.1mph, setting a new speed record in the races.

Crewe's Improved Precedents could not only reach high speeds but regularly hauled heavy loads in relation to their small size, hence their nickname 'Jumbo'.

In June 1896, the rivals agreed a minimum journey time for daytime trains, but the sky was still the limit for those at night.

However, on July 13, 1896, the 8pm 'Highland Express' from Euston to Scotland spectacularly derailed to the north of Preston station in the middle of the night, killing one of its 16 passengers. Scheduled to maintain an average speed of 60mph for 105 miles of its journey, relying on razor-sharp enginemanship especially at night, it had defied a 10mph restriction to take a curve at 40-45mph.

SLOWDOWN

Following the bad publicity generated by the crash, the public mood towards racing trains changed to one of hostility, and safety regained

Preserved No. 6100 *Royal Scot* in action during the Steel, Steam & Stars II gala at the Llangollen Railway in April 2009. The locomotive is running without smoke deflectors, as did the members of the original class until 1931. ROBIN JONES

top priority. Indeed, when the Great Western Railway's No. 3440 *City of Truro* supposedly became the first in the world to break the 100mph barrier, unofficially touching 102.3mph with the 'Ocean Mails' on Wellington Bank in Somerset in May 1904, the company kept quiet about it for many years afterwards.

After the Preston accident, the east and west coast companies reached agreement on limiting speeds. London to Scotland journey times would remain at the 1889 timing of around eight hours well into the 1930s as a result.

However, for its summer 1901 service, the Midland and North British railways announced that the 9.30am St Pancras express on the Settle and Carlisle and Waverley lines would arrive in Edinburgh at 6.05pm, 10 minutes before the Great Northern, North British and North Eastern railways' 'Flying Scotsman'. Worried that a delayed Midland train might lead to Portobello East junction becoming like

Kinnaber, NER rescheduled its train for 6.02pm and then earlier, ignoring the 1896 agreement. Both the Caledonian and the North Eastern railways ran fast trains in retaliation for a few days, but the North British backed down.

BIG ENGINES, LITTLE ONES

Fast forward to 1921, when the government merged more than 120 separate railways companies into four. The move came about because of the benefits that were seen in running the country's railways as a single entity during the First World War, but the government of David Lloyd George stopped short of permanent nationalisation.

Many of the pre-Grouping railways ran services and routes also offered by their rivals, with the result that both made losses.

In the build-up to the enforced creation of the Big Four, the LNWR merged with the Lancashire & Yorkshire Railway from January

1, 1922. The merged company became the biggest constituent of the London, Midland & Scottish Railway when it was formed on New Year's Day 1923.

Brought into the LMS was the Caledonian Railway, placing the west coast route under one owner for the first time. The Grouping also saw the three constituent companies of the east coast route become the backbone of the London & North Eastern Railway.

As well as the Furness, Glasgow & South Western, Highland, North Staffordshire railways and three companies in Northern Ireland, the LNWR's old rival the Midland came into the fold.

The LMS was the world's largest transport organisation, the biggest commercial undertaking in the British Empire and Britain's second largest employer after the Post Office. By 1938, it operated 6870 miles of railway on the British mainland.

Josiah Stamp, who later became director of the Bank of England, was appointed as the first president of the LMS executive. However, the upper tiers of the company management were filled largely with Midland Railway men who were determined to continue the Derby tradition, irrespective of practicalities.

The Midland's crimson-lake livery became the LMS standard. That was not a problem – but the Midland's 'little engine' policy certainly was.

The west coast operators had built big powerful engines with raw power to tackle gradients such as Shap and Beattock with heavy loads, while the Midland, with its gentler gradients and more stopping places, coped with smaller locomotives. They often had to double head heavier trains, especially on the Settle and Carlisle line.

There was a dramatic contrast between the powerful LNWR classes such as the George the Fifth 4-4-0s and Midland Railway chief mechanical engineer Richard Deeley's 4-4-0

Caledonian Railway 8ft 2in wheeled 2-2-2 No. 87. This class was introduced in 1859 onwards and served as the main express engine until 1885. The last of the class was withdrawn from service in 1901. TONY HISGETT COLLECTION*

Crewe station in pre-1900 LNWR days. TONY HISGETT COLLECTION*

compounds, which weighed the same but had far less power.

More and shorter trains had to be run on the Midland routes, while paths had to be created for locomotives running light engine back to base after double heading or banking duties. The policy was ridiculed thus:

M is for Midland with engines galore
Two on each train and asking for more

Yet even some of the bigger LNWR locomotives struggled, having to run longer distances on a unified West Coast Main Line. Double heading was needed north of Preston with the Scottish express.

However, lessons were not being learned. Derby continued to build smaller engines, such as Class 2P 4-4-0s and 0-6-0 freight engines. Older designs were modified in a bid to tackle the power shortfall.

The doubling up of locomotives on the west coast route led to extra staffing costs and lower profits. The situation was highlighted when the prestigious 'Royal Scot' 15-coach train from Euston to Glasgow was introduced in the summer of 1927. It had to be hauled by an LNWR Claughton assisted by a George the Fifth or Precursor south of Carnforth, before being hauled by a pair of new compounds over Shap.

The answer was obvious – build one locomotive to do the job.

Yet George Hughes, who had been inherited by the Lancashire & Yorkshire, was replaced on his retirement in 1925 as chief mechanical engineer by Sir Henry Fowler, who had been partially responsible for the small-engine policy.

Fowler brought out the first standard LMS design, the 2-6-0 'Crab' type, of which 135 were built. In fairness, he recognised the inadequacies on the west coast route, and in 1926 began designing a compound Pacific express locomotive, only to be met with a lack of internal support.

Instead, the LMS board opted for a three-cylinder 4-6-0 largely inspired by GWR 4-6-0 No. 5000 *Launceston Castle*, which had been borrowed for a month to test out between Euston and Carlisle. Adapting elements from the Southern Railway's Lord Nelson 4-6-0s and Fowler's 2-6-4

tank engine, the Royal Scot emerged.

The first of this new breed of 4-6-0s appeared in 1927. They proved to be outstanding, capable of hauling 420-ton trains by themselves over Shap and Beattock, and were immediately allocated to the top LMS expresses.

No. 6100 was selected as the sole British exhibit at the great Chicago Exhibition of 1933, which was held on the theme of A Century of Progress. An entire 'Royal Scot' train was shipped to North America for the show.

Before and after the exhibition, the train toured the United States and Canada, highlighting British engineering at its very best.

The engine operated in incredible temperatures ranges – from 110°F in the shade, to 26°F below freezing, performing better than trains which had been purpose-built for the Rocky Mountains and the North American conditions. The tour began on April 21 and finished in a snowstorm 11,194 miles later on November 11, when the train arrived at Montreal two minutes early.

A true classic had been created, but there were LMS directors who wanted more – in the shape of a GWR Castle. The GWR refused to sell them one or even loan the drawings, but there were other means to the end. ∎

Driver John Souter examines Caledonian Railway No. 17 at the end of its record run with the last leg of the Euston to Aberdeen train on August 23, 1895. The picture was issued as a hand-coloured postcard by the railway for publicity purposes.

CHAPTER TWO

HEADHUNTED
FOR GLORY

William Henry Stanier was born in Wolverhampton on April 28, 1849. When he was old enough, he joined the Great Western Railway works in the town as an office boy.

He thrived in the role, earning promotion and eventually becoming clerk to the works' locomotive superintendent William Dean.

When Dean was made assistant to GWR locomotive superintendent Joseph Armstrong at Swindon, he thought so highly of Stanier that he asked him to accompany him there as his chief clerk.

Armstrong died suddenly in 1877, and Dean was promoted to the top job.

By then, W H Stanier had married, and the first of his six children, William Arthur Stanier, was born on May 27, 1876 – the year in which Alexander Graham Bell produced his first telephone.

With the backing of Dean, the enterprising William Henry set up a laboratory for chemical and mechanical testing of samples for the works, at the family's home, Oakfields in The Sands. He also ran technical education classes for Swindon apprentices at the town's GWR Mechanics Institute.

With the laboratory in the house, his son took an interest in mechanical matters.

He was educated at Swindon High School, and aged 10, he was given his first set of chisels.

In January 1891, he was sent to Wycliffe College, a boarding school near Stonehouse in Gloucestershire, but despite achieving well academically, returned permanently to Swindon that Christmas.

His father found him a job as an office boy in Swindon Works, and the following May, he became an apprentice at the age of 16. A week after his birthday, he started in the carriage

works, at a time when the last broad gauge trains had run and the 7ft 0¼in gauge had to be either converted to standard gauge or scrapped.

By late 1893, young William had graduated to the fitting shop, and in November that year, was transferred to the locomotive works. During a 21-month placement in the fitting and machine shops he learned many new skills.

In the summer of 1895, William moved to the erecting shop, and was able to accompany new locomotives on their trial runs. At the same time, he attended engineering classes in the Mechanics Institute, determined to make the most of every opportunity that came his way.

May 1897 marked the start of a stint in the pattern shop, and on November 1, he entered the Drawing Office, having been given a junior draughtsman's job in the carriage and wagon section.

LMS Princess Royal Pacific No. 6201 *Princess Elizabeth* takes the Golden Valley line at Standish Junction with the Royal Train carrying the Queen and Duke of Edinburgh from Newport to Hereford and Worcester to Oxford on July 11, 2012. Run as part of the Queen's Diamond Jubilee celebrations, it was believed to be the first time that the Queen had ridden on a train hauled by the Stanier locomotive named after her. PETE BERRY

William Henry Stanier, who found his son his first job at Swindon. GWR

Sir William Stanier in 1941.

The teenage William Stanier joined the GWR at a seminal moment in the company's history; the conversion of the last broad gauge lines to standard gauge in 1892. At Swindon he would have viewed the 15 miles of sidings of redundant locomotives, carriages and wagons that no longer had any track on which to run, and were awaiting the cutter's torch. GWR

RISING THROUGH THE RANKS

On January 9, 1899, he moved to the Locomotive Drawing Office, where he attracted the attention of the new assistant chief draughtsman, Charles B Collett.

On March 1, 1900, he became inspector of materials at the GWR's Birmingham and Manchester Districts. The following year, backed by Dean, William Stanier the younger became an associate member of the Institution of Mechanical Engineers, later on, in 1908 becoming a full member.

He continued to climb the ladder and in September 1901 became a mechanical inspector at Swindon locomotive shed. January 11, 1904, saw him become assistant divisional superintendent at Westbourne Park shed near Paddington.

He was transferred back to Swindon in April, 1906, firstly as assistant works manager,

and then, in November, as locomotive, carriage and wagon superintendent of the Swindon Division. In between, that July, he married Ella Morse, daughter of Levi Lapper Morse, who later became MP for South Wiltshire.

At Swindon, William Stanier took a hands-on role with all of the ground-breaking locomotives designed by Dean's successor, George Jackson Churchward, who is widely regarded as not only the finest chief mechanical engineer of the GWR, but of any railway in Britain.

Churchward took the GWR out of the era of oversize brass domes, stovepipe chimneys, single driving wheels and minimalists cabs, while resisting the temptation of experimenting with electric or other modes of traction, as was the case elsewhere.

William Stanier rode on the new locomotive types such as the Saint and Star 4-6-0s, and

even drove some of them. He would have been well acquainted with the first Pacific to be built in Britain, Churchward's No. 111 *The Great Bear*, which emerged from Swindon Works in February 1908.

The 4-6-2 took the term Pacific from the USA where manufacturer Baldwin had supplied them to the Missouri Pacific Railroad.

Churchward wanted to demonstrate that it was possible to build a four-cylinder locomotive with 15in diameter cylinders which could be adequately fed by a standard GWR boiler.

The Great Bear experienced early problems with clearance on curves and springing of the trailing wheels. Modifications were also made to the superheating of the boiler.

Its size and axle loading gauge meant that *The Great Bear* was all but exclusively restricted to the Paddington to Bristol line.

A 36-ton breakdown crane demonstrates its power by lifting Britain's first Pacific, No. 111 *The Great Bear*. Probably built more for prestige than anything, its designer George Jackson Churchward did not develop the project into a production class. After he retired, he was told that Gresley was planning to build a Pacific for the Great Northern Railway. "What did that young man want to build it for?" he exclaimed. "We could have sold him ours!"

GWR Castle 4-6-0 No. 5043 Earl of Mount Edgcumbe stands at the Paddington buffer stops with Tyseley-based Vintage Trains' rerun of the 'Cheltenham Flyer' on May 11, 2013. ROBIN JONES

A classic example of what has been described as possibly the finest of all British mixed traffic locomotives: LMS 'Black Five' 4-6-0 No. 45305 ascends the 1-in-50 climb out of Garve on the Kyle of Lochalsh line with the Railway Touring Company's 'Great Britain V' railtour on April 23, 2014. BRIAN SHARPE

There is no doubt that Churchward, given the chance, would probably have improved on the design, and within a decade, the flagship of the Swindon empire might well have been a fleet of Pacifics.

However, with Swindon Works diverting his attention to supplying military needs during the First World War, and Churchward concentrating on advancing the development of his 4-6-0s, taking *The Great Bear* to the next stage was not considered a priority.

In January 1924, *The Great Bear*, then needing heavy repairs to its boiler after just 527,272 miles, was dismantled and the parts used to build one of Churchward's successor Collett's Castle class 4-6-0s.

In 1911, William Stanier was involved in the design of Churchward's 43XX class of mixed traffic 2-6-0s. Late the following year, he was promoted to the position of assistant (senior) locomotive works manager, under Collett. His father, W H Stanier, retired in 1914.

WORKS MANAGER AND BEYOND

In 1920, Stanier was promoted to the post of works manager, when Collett became assistant chief mechanical engineer, and then, on Churchward's retirement the following year, CME.

As works manager, Stanier found himself at the heart of a major expansion programme at

Swindon, one which would turn it into the most updated locomotive works in Britain.

Collett then appointed Stanier as his assistant.

Unlike Churchward, Collett was no inventor – but the GWR's greatest innovator. He took the magnificent designs that he had inherited to the next logical stages of development.

In doing so, Collett produced the finest and most powerful GWR locomotives of all time.

At the Grouping of 1923, the GWR empire was swelled by the addition of 560 miles of track, 18,000 employees and a further 700 locomotives, many of them decidedly nonstandard and therefore not wanted in the medium to long term by the Swindon empire.

What was needed was not someone to produce a new generation of world beaters as a priority, but who would build on what had been achieved so far, while modernising production and cutting costs.

When a more powerful locomotive class than the Stars was demanded, Collett enlarged the Star boiler to give a greater evaporative rate, increased the diameter of the cylinders and raised the nominal tractive effort to 31,625lb.

The result was a Castle 4-6-0 – announced by the GWR publicity department as the most powerful locomotive in the UK when it was launched.

The Castles had been made possible by Collett's improved workshop practices and methods at Swindon, cutting costs while bettering existing designs. However, in the wake of the sudden death of Collett's wife after a short illness, much of the development work on the class was delegated to Stanier.

Among the Castles' finest moments were their performances on the 'Cheltenham Spa Express'. When they entered service on the Paddington to Cheltenham route in 1923, an average speed of 61.8mph cut the timings from Swindon to Paddington by 10 minutes to 75.

The negative public mood in the wake of the Preston 1896 train crash largely forgotten, by the late Twenties, the Big Four began competing in terms of speed once more.

On June 6, 1932, on the Cheltenham route, a new speed record was set of 56 minutes 47 seconds from Swindon to Paddington, at an average speed of 81.6mph, by No. 5006 *Tregenna Castle*. What was now the fastest railway run in the world earned the train the nickname of the 'Cheltenham Flyer'.

In September that year, the schedule for the Swindon to Paddington journey was set at 65 minutes, giving an average speed of 71.3mph. It was the first time in railway history that any train had been scheduled at more than 70mph.

The next stage of development was Collett's King 4-6-0, the ultimate GWR flagship. Stanier

oversaw an all-out effort to complete the first of the class, No. 6000 *King George V*, for a trial run on the 'Cornish Riviera Express' on July 20, 1927, a few days before it was shipped, on August 3, to the US to take part on the centenary celebrations for the Baltimore & Ohio Railway, accompanied by Stanier.

Around this time, Sir Henry Fowler of the LMS had taken Stanier and Gresley to Euston to see what he described as "the finest engine in the British Isles" – No. 6100 *Royal Scot*. Stanier, proud of his company's new king, replied disparagingly: "Or anyway, the finest smokebox."

THE ULTIMATE CAREER MOVE

Excellent as the Royal Scots might be, the LMS did not own a single locomotive capable of hauling a 500-ton express by itself all 401 miles from Euston to Glasgow.

Despite the GWR's stout refusal, the directors wanted to have a Castle at all costs.

Having their bid to buy one or more turned down by Swindon, and then being refused access to the drawings, there was one trick still up their sleeve. Poach the designer, or at least his right-hand man.

After the trip to the US, the 52-year-old Stanier probably thought himself too old to ever step into Collett's shoes should he retire, as he was just five years younger.

Sir Josiah Stamp – the LMS chairman who headhunted William Stanier from the GWR.

However, in 1932, Stanier was approached by LMS chairman, Sir Josiah Stamp, who invited him to become the new chief mechanical engineer of the LMS, and handed him the task of ridding the company of the Midland Railway small-engine policy and designing new modern and far more powerful locomotives.

The post had become available after Fowler was moved sideways in 1930 to the LMS Research Department, briefly replaced by Ernest Lemon, Derby's divisional carriage and wagon superintendent. Within a year, Lemon was shifted upstairs to make way for Stanier, who joined on January 1, 1932.

The appointment was one of the most far-sighted and indeed spectacular in railway history.

One of his most successful LMS designs was the 'Black Five' mixed traffic 4-6-0, which has been described as the best all-purpose steam locomotive ever to appear on Britain's railways. With the 'Black Fives' Stanier drew upon design elements of the GWR Hall 4-6-0s.

The class was so successful that several lasted until the end of British Railways steam haulage in August 1968, and 18 have been preserved.

Between 1934 and 1936, 191 of Stanier's Jubilee 4-6-0s were built at Derby and Crewe by the North British Locomotive Company. Indeed, the last five of Fowler's Patriot 4-6-0s, a smaller version of the Royal Scots, had Stanier's taper boiler added to become Jubilees, so named after the Silver Jubilee of King George V in 1935.

Another stunner was Stanier's 8F 2-8-0, a freight version of the 'Black Five'. A total of 852 were built, with the locomotive works of other Big Four companies turning them out for the War Department and service overseas during the Second World War.

If Stanier had stopped there, he would have been immortalised among the greatest railway engineers by his designs, all of which deserve a book or two, or three, in their own right. However, his finest hour was yet to come.

THE RACES ARE BACK ON

It was the LNER, the great rival of the LMS, that was to follow on from *The Great Bear* and build Pacifics for use in Britain.

In 1911, Nigel Gresley was made chief mechanical engineer of the Great Northern Railway. Inspired by the Pennsylvania Railroad's new K4 4-6-2s, built his first two Pacifics in 1922, No. 1470 *Great Northern*, and No. 1471 *Sir Frederick*, with the aim of producing a locomotive that could haul longer trains than Henry Ivatt's large Atlantics, which had began the GNR's big engine policy when they appeared in 1902.

Utilising Gresley's universal three-cylinder layout from two of his earlier designs, his Pacifics made full use of the maximum limits of the East Coast Main Line loading gauge with large boilers and wide round-topped fireboxes providing a large grate area. Heat transfer and the flow of gases were aided by a combustion chamber which extended forward from the firebox space into the boiler barrel.

Gresley's GNR Pacific became the standard LNER express passenger locomotive and was designated Class A1, with a total of 51 built. With the LNER after 1923 controlling the entire ECML, not just the GNR section, locomotives that could work longer distances were required, just as the LMS needed bigger engines for Euston to Glasgow.

A1 No. 1472 was renumbered 4472 and named *Flying Scotsman* before being displayed at the British Empire Exhibition at Wembley along with the GWR's No. 4073 *Caerphilly Castle*. Two months after the 1924 event, the GWR and LNER held exchange trials to see who had the best locomotive, and sister No. 4079 *Pendennis Castle* came out on top.

Examining data from the trials, Gresley modified his A1s, designing a similar but superior Pacific, the A3, and eventually

MAP
OF THE
LMS RAILWAY
1938

Places with LMS Hotels shown thus GLENEAGLES

The GWR publicity department made much of the 'Cheltenham Flyer' being the world's fastest train, which led to other Big Four companies scrapping decades-old agreements against 'racing' trains, such as those from London to Scotland. **ROBIN JONES**

upgrading all the A1s into A3s with modified valve gear.

The modifications led to coal consumption being drastically reduced, making it possible to run the 'Flying Scotsman' service from King's Cross to Edinburgh nonstop with a heavy train on one tender full of coal. They were provided with corridor tenders to allow the crew to be changed mid-journey.

Flying Scotsman the locomotive was used to haul the inaugural nonstop train from London on May 1, 1928, completing all 393 miles without stopping, a record at the time for a scheduled service.

However, four days earlier, the LMS had run the 'Royal Scot' all 399.7 miles from Euston to Edinburgh nonstop as a publicity stunt, using Royal Scot No. 6113 *Cameronian* fitted with an ex-Midland Railway tender with extended coal rails to Glasgow and a 4P compound on the Edinburgh portion, in a bid to upstage the LNER.

The speed limitation agreement which had remained in place between the east and west coast operators since the last Race to the North in 1895 was torn up in 1932.

That year, the LNER brought the 'Flying Scotsman' journey time down to seven hours 30 minutes, and to seven hours 20 minutes by 1938.

On November 30, 1934, *Flying Scotsman* set a new world record when it was officially recorded reaching 100mph just outside Little

The greatest challenge to the LMS on the London to Scotland routes was the emergence of Gresley's streamlined A4 Pacifics. The first A4, No. 2509, which set a new record on its press run, is seen at Grantham in June 1937. **J WHALEY/COLOUR RAIL**

Bytham while descending Stoke Bank in Lincolnshire with a six-coach test train between Leeds and London. The LNER sought to make the most of it.

The Races to the North had by then been yanked into the 20th century. In the aftermath of the 1929 Wall Street Crash, Britain was trying to dispel the gloom of a recession, while the railway companies needed to boost

income. One targeted area was the long-distance expresses such as the London to Scotland routes.

At the LMS, Stanier's programme included the building of three prototype Pacifics. The first, No. 6200 *The Princess Royal*, was completed on June 27, 1933, and led to two batches of locomotives being built. There was a first batch of two, including No. 6201

GWR 4-6-0 No. 5000 *Launceston Castle* – pictured at Denham in the Fifties – was hired by the LMS for a month, at a time when it desperately needed adequate motive power for the West Coast Main Line runs from Euston to Scotland.

Another major Stanier classic was the LMS Jubilee 4-6-0. No. 45593 *Kolhapur*, one of four examples to be preserved. It is seen on the turntable at its Tyseley Locomotive Works home on June 25, 2011, during an open weekend. ROBIN JONES

Princess Elizabeth, and a second batch of 11. The official name for the class was selected because Mary, the Princess Royal, was the commander-in-chief of the Royal Scots. However, class members were soon nicknamed 'Lizzies' after No. 6201.

Meanwhile, events on the continent were sounding alarm bells. In 1933, the German state railway Deutsche Reichsbahn-Gesellschaft launched its 'Flying Hamburger' 98-seater two-car high-speed streamlined diesel railcar on the Berlin-Hamburg line, where it recorded an average speed of 77.4mph over the 178-mile journey.

Gresley rode on it and was impressed. It seemed that the curtain was about to descend on the steam age, but Sir Ralph Wedgwood, the LNER's chief general manager, then suggested that faster overall speeds might be achieved with a Pacific.

THE ADVENT OF STREAMLINING

In 1933, the launch of the 'Flying Hamburger' high-speed diesel railcar set in Germany made worldwide headlines.

It seemed that the steam age was over.

Yet the LNER decided that while diesel power might well be the future, steam still ruled the roost, and under the right conditions, could produce high speeds.

The fastest train in Britain in the early Thirties was the GWR's 'Cheltenham Spa Express', which was hauled by Castles, averaging 71.3mph between Swindon and Paddington.

LNER chief mechanical engineer Nigel Gresley – who in 1893 had been apprenticed as a premium pupil of Francis Webb at Crewe – set out to introduce a new, long-distance, high-speed train service on the East Coast Main Line in 1935.

On November 30, 1934, No. 4472 *Flying Scotsman* reached 100mph, the first steam locomotive in the world officially to do so, on Stoke Bank in Lincolnshire during a test run between Leeds and King's Cross. On the outward trip to Leeds, with renowned driver William Sparshatt in charge, No. 4472 had taken four coaches 185.8 miles from King's Cross to Leeds in 151 minutes six seconds.

Forgetting the reservations shown by the GWR about revealing *City of Truro*'s unofficial 102.3mph feat in 1904, the LNER threw caution to the winds and maximised publicity from the event.

In March 1935, A3 No. 2750 *Papyrus* with six coaches ran from King's Cross to Newcastle and back. The 500 miles were covered in 423 minutes 23 seconds, including 300 miles at 80mph average, and reaching 108mph at one point – setting a new world record.

Data collected from the run paved the way for Gresley's next development of his A3s, in the form of the streamlined A4, which had a higher boiler pressure, at 250psi, and slightly reduced cylinder diameter, to give greater power.

That in itself was a leap forward, but in the eyes of the public it was the revolutionary shape of the locomotive that at first generated much debate.

The world had never seen the like of it before. The striking appearance was inspired by a Bugatti railcar, which in turn mirrored that of one of the Italian manufacturer's racing cars. And race it would.

Appearing in the art deco era, the shape was, however, designed to be far more than cosmetic.

The streamlining had been subjected to wind tunnel testing at the National Physical Laboratory in Teddington, aiming to make the most of aerodynamics to enhance speed, and in so doing keeping ahead not only of the Germans but the LMS too – although historians and engineers have often debated as to whether streamlining steam locomotives really made any significant difference to their performance.

The A4s were designed to work the 'Silver Jubilee', a train of seven matching streamlined coaches, covering the 232.3 miles from Darlington to King's Cross at an average of 70.4mph. A press run was staged on September 27, 1935, heading by the

LMS Stanier 8F No. 8274 at Winchcombe with a freight train on May 25, 2014, during the Cotswold Festival of Steam on the Gloucestershire Warwickshire Railway. No. 8274 was built by North British (Works No. 24648) in 1940 for the War Department as an 'interim austerity' locomotive and numbered 348, but it was initially loaned to the LMS as No.8274. However, after only a few weeks, it was taken back by the WD, but after the fall of France it was no longer needed. After the war it was sold by the WD to TCDD (Turkish State Railways) as No.45160. It was repatriated to the UK in 1989 for restoration and steamed on the Swanage Railway that year, before being stopped for an overhaul that took more 20 years. ROBIN JONES

One of the Churchward classes on which William Stanier worked at Swindon was the 43XX mixed traffic mogul. He once described it as the "engine of the future" noting that it was suitable for working both excursion traffic and troop trains. One of two surviving examples out of a total of 342, 1917-built No. 5322, is seen at Didcot Railway Centre on May 1, 2011, having been repainted into ROD khaki livery to commemorate its role overseas in the latter part of the First World War, along with 19 other class members. MARTIN ROBSON*

freshly out-of-the-works Gresley A4 No. 2509 *Silver Link*.

On the trip, Silver Link entered the legend category by twice reaching 112mph, snatching the world record away from Papyrus, while trials with increased loadings on August 27, 1936, saw sister streamliner A4 No. 2512 *Silver Fox* hit 113mph while going down Stoke Bank,

setting a new British record for a passenger service train.

There was now a clear road ahead for the LNER's next streamlined train, the 'Coronation', to reduce the King's Cross to Edinburgh journey time to six hours with one stop.

Gresley and the LNER had thrown down the gauntlet to Stanier and his employers.■

CHAPTER THREE

DRIVER TOM CLARK
CORONATION AND CROCKERY

A contemporary hand-coloured view of *LMS Princess Coronation Pacific* No. 6220 Coronation leaving London for Crewe with the 'Coronation Scot' preview run on June 29, 1937, that would claim a 114mph British steam record, even though the crockery in the dining car did not come out of it too well.

Just as in the Races to the North, the west coast operator would respond to the east coast challenge.

However, such competition could never be a level playing field.

The LNER had the advantage of the fairly flat and straight East Coast Main Line, allowing it to operate very successful short-formation and lightweight high-speed trains.

By contrast, the LMS was faced with the demanding gradients of Shap and Beattock over which its locomotives had to haul 600 ton trains of up to 17 coaches.

Stanier's team drew up plans for a six hour nonstop service between Euston and Glasgow Central to rival the LNER's similarly timed services, and set a new Anglo-Scottish record.

On paper it seemed feasible, but a trial run had to take place to prove it could be done.

Tom Clark, the senior driver from 5A Crewe North shed, from where locomen worked south to London and north to Perth was chosen. He would be assisted by fireman Charles Fleet and passed fireman Albert Shaw.

Clark had signed up to the LNWR in December 1888 and risen through the ranks from cleaner to driver at Crewe North. Somewhat mirroring William Stanier, his best came in the final years of his career.

Princess Royal Pacific No. 6201 *Princess Elizabeth* was rostered to run the test train from Euston to Glasgow Central.

The '5A Three' travelled to London the night before the special run, lodging with other engine men in the noisy and not select in any way railwaymen's 'barracks' at Camden shed.

On November 16, 1936, Tom Clark and his crew drove the train, designated 703, and weighting 225 tons, from Euston to Glasgow in five hours 53 minutes 38 seconds. It was the longest nonstop journey with a steam locomotive that had been performed at that time. The average speed had been 68.3mph, while for a mile between Tring and Bletchley, the train reached 95mph. Shap was conquered at 58.5mph: indeed, all speed records for the West Coast Main Line were broken by the train.

A reporter on the northbound train threw out a message at Carlisle station which read: "Intense excitement for the last lap with the 1-in-69 gradient of Beattock ahead. Beating schedule and 90mph frequently exceeded.

"Despite terrific speed, train riding beautifully. Crowds waving us on at every station, and at one wayside station a notice, 'It's in your pocket' waved from the platform."

The LMS chief officer for Scotland, Mr J Ballantyne, remarked: "It is possible that, as a result of this, we shall have a permanent train doing the journey from London to Glasgow."

Next day, the trio completed the return journey in five hours 44 minutes 14 seconds. Nonstop Glasgow Central to Euston was

First of the class: Princess Coronation Pacific No. 6220 *Coronation* leaving Crewe Works in 1937. NRM

accomplished at an average speed of 69mph, with an average load of 240 tons. It was the fastest run between Scotland and England.

On arrival back at Euston, the footplate trio were taken to Broadcasting House and interviewed by the BBC. There, they were feted as national heroes.

Newspaper front page headlines such '401 Miles Non Stop', 'Railway Ambition Achieved', and 'London-Glasgow Under Six Hours' fired volleys of warning shorts over the LNER's bows.

The LMS directors and their chief mechanical engineer knew that they were right to produce the blueprint for a new Anglo-Scottish express, to be named the ' Coronation Scot'.

Suddenly, every schoolboy in Britain wanted to be the next Tom Clark. Model railway manufacturer Hornby immediately produced an O gauge model of No. 6201 in the wake of its feat.

When it was officially launched on May 1, 1937, Hornby arranged for a photograph to be staged at Edge Hill depot, Liverpool with two schoolboys holding a model alongside the full-size locomotive, together with Tom Clark and Fleet. Clark was reported as having said, "It's grand," a well-known Crewe phrase.

Mention must also be made of the third prototype Princess Royal Pacific, No. 6202, the unnamed 'Turbomotive'. Built with the aid of the Swedish Ljungstrom turbine company and numbered 6202, in sequence with the other Princess Royals, it had a larger 40 element superheater to give a higher steam temperature, more suitable for turbine use. The boiler was also domeless, as would be the case with the second batch of the Princess Royals. The continuous exhaust of the turbine, rather than the sharper intermittent blast of the piston engine, also required changes to the draughting and the use of a double chimney.

It entered service in June 1935 on the London-Liverpool service, and was rebuilt as a conventional locomotive in 1952 and named *Princess Anne*, but was then destroyed in the Harrow & Wealdstone train crash months later.

The appearance of such an experimental locomotive was another indication that Stanier was not prepared to rest on his laurels with the Princess Royals, especially as he and the LMS board knew only too well that Gresley would respond – not just to retake the British speed record, but maybe the world record too.

For six months before 'Lizzie's' stupendous run, on May 11, 1936, one of three Borsig-built Class 05 4-6-4s, No. 05003 reached 124.5mph while hauling a 194 ton train on the flat line between Berlin and Hamburg.

It had not been an intentional record run, but a VIP special for Nazi top brass, organised in response to the concern of German railway officials that Hitler would favour autobahns as the way ahead rather than rail.

After a series of red signals slowed the special down on the last lap home, officials feared that the guests would become irritated, and so the footplate crew was told to give it everything they had – setting a speed record in the process. Perhaps they and the world had everything to fear, for on board were Heinrich Himmler and Reinhard Heydrich, two main architects of the Holocaust, which relied mainly on railways to transport millions of innocent people to their deaths.

Hornby's advertisement for its new model of No. 6201 *Princess Elizabeth* featured driver Tom Clark (left) and his fireman Tom Fleet, who by then had become national heroes and role models for the prewar generation.

The doors of the streamlined casing of the first Princess Coronation Pacific, No. 6220 *Coronation*, seen in the fully-open position on May 15, 1937, at Crewe Works. NRM

THE FIRST OF THE 'BIG LIZZIES'

In a bid to take the British speed record, Stanier looked at building on the success of his Princess Royals, by designing what was in effect enlarged version to match or even better the A4s.

Taking a leaf from Gresley's glamorous A4s, he added streamlining to the design.

The result: the first of 38 new streamlined Princess Coronation class Pacifics, No. 6220 *Coronation*, which emerged from Crewe Works on June 1, 1937.

At 3300hp, they were the most powerful passenger steam locomotives ever built for the British railway network.

The detail design work was carried out by Tom Coleman, the LMS chief draftsman, Stanier's personal assistant Robert Riddles and Crewe Works manager Roland Bond.

The Princess Coronation class tenders were fitted with a steam-operated coal pusher to bring the coal down to the firing plate. That would aid firemen to meet the high demands for power during the nonstop run of 299 miles between Euston and Carlisle on the 'Royal Scot' bound for Glasgow Central.

The first five Princess Coronations, Nos. 6220-4, all of which were allocated to Camden shed, were fitted with a trademark bulbous art deco casing and painted Caledonian Railway blue with silver horizontal lines to match the 'Coronation Scot' train that they were built to haul. The wheels, lining to the edges of the bands, and the background to the chromium-plated nameplates were painted in a darker blue. The styling of the streamlined casing was influenced by German and American designs such as the Class 05 and the New York Central Railroad's K5 4-6-2.

Again, as was the case with the A4s, critics have argued the casings of both had more to do with style rather than substance, and claimed it made no difference at speeds lower than 90mph.

Just as Gresley had ordered wind tunnel testing to find the most optimum wedge shape for his A4s, so scale models of the Princess Coronations were tested in the wind tunnel at the LMS Scientific Research Laboratory in Derby.

A model made to Coleman's design showed that the bulbous front end disturbed the air less than the A4's wedge, but the downside was that there would be less clearance of exhaust gases, and smoke drifting into the driver's line of vision.

And who would be chosen to drive *Coronation* on a preview run to reclaim the British record from the LNER? None other than Tom Clark.

On Tuesday June 29, 1937, with a press trip before the official launch of the 'Coronation Scot' a week later, No. 6220, with Clark's hand on the regulator, assisted by freman J Lewis, covered the 158 miles from Euston to Crewe in two hours nine minutes 45 seconds, reclaiming the British record with a top speed of 114mph.

The run began on Madeley bank, nine miles south of the great railway town. The bank, offered 1¾ miles at 1-in-177 immediately after Whitmore summit, and 2¾ miles at 1-in-69, ending 1¼ miles south of Crewe station.

The speed had not topped 87.5mph until the train had passed Whitmore, where the footplate

LMS Princess Royal 4-6-2 No. 6201 *Princess Elizabeth,* **a record setting which paved the way for the Princess Coronation Pacifics, passes Wavertree with a Liverpool to west of England express in 1938.** ERIC TREACY / *THE RAILWAY MAGAZINE*

crew decided not to pick up water from the troughs so as to avoid having to slow down.

They took the summit at 85mph, and as No. 6220 descended Madeley bank, speed increased to 108mph at Betley Road.

The 114mph, taken by Riddles from the locomotive's speed indicator, was claimed just before milepost 156, just south of Crewe, although some experts said that 113mph, the same as the LNER record, was more probably the correct figure, as the speed indicator was not usually considered sufficiently accurate for detailed timings.

Seasoned observer Cecil J Allen was on board alongside other timing experts, and none recorded anything higher than 112.5mpm, at mileposts 155 and 156. However, it was considered possible that 113mph was reached in between.

This outward trip ended with a hair-raising experience, when Clark did not allow adequate braking distance before the 20mph limit on a reverse curve on the approach to Crewe.

Approaching Crewe, the train was still travelling at the top speed, with spectators from the town gathering on the lineside. Clark applied the brakes, but the train sped on with flames leaping from the brake blocks, according to Riddles who was on board.

No. 6220 was travelling at 60-70mph when it approached the Crewe platform 3 signal, he said.

Famously, crockery in the dining car was sent crashing to the floor before Clark slowed down to around 60mph and then 52mph on the first of three reverse curves on a trackwork complex with a series of crossovers.

Standing passengers were flung off their feet, although none were injured apart from bruising, and a few of the rail chairs were also damaged.

Yet he still brought the train to a standstill

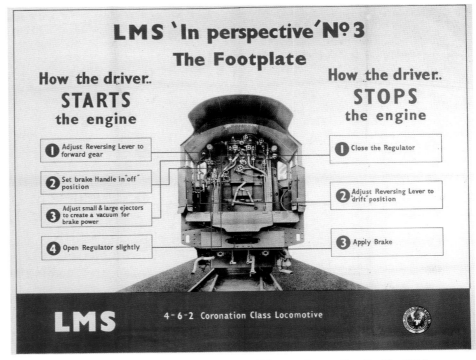

A diagrammatic explanation of the control of a Princess Coronation Pacific. NRM

at Crewe, with the locomotive and all of the carriages still on the rails.

His derring-do proved that both the Princess Coronation and the permanent way could handle it. It was said that the stability of No. 6220 on the occasion had more to do with the design of the leading Churchward De Glehn bogie than the driver's abilities.

Clark said afterwards: "With the engine riding like the great lady she is there wasn't a thing we could do about it but hold on and let her take it."

The last 10½ miles from Whitmore to Crewe

had been covered in just under seven minutes. The overall time from Euston was 129.75 minutes at an average speed of 73.1mph, with the final 1.1 miles to Crewe station achieved in one minute 19 seconds.

At the ensuing press lunch, LMS vice-president Sir Ernest Lemon told those in attendance: "Of course gentlemen, you realise that we shan't need to do this kind of thing on every trip of the 'Coronation Scot'; we were coming in a little faster than we shall have to, in the ordinary course.'

The return trip from Crewe back to Euston

The plaque on the side of the streamlined casing of A4 No. 4468 *Mallard* which proudly displays its unbeaten 126mph world speed record. ROBIN JONES

took 119 minutes, an average of 79.7mph, one of the fastest ever recorded in Britain.

On this leg, the 69.9 miles from Walton to Willesden Junction was covered in a spectacular 47 minutes one second, at an average of 89.3mph, with a maximum speed of 100mph recorded at Castlethorpe water troughs. The train arrived back at Euston early, having cut 16 minutes off the journey.

The company wasted no time in claiming the fastest start-to-stop runs of over 100 and 150 miles.

But there was no way that it was going to rest there, for the next day, the LNER hit back.

A4 No. 4489 *Dominion of Canada* was rostered for the trial run of the 'Coronation', the LNER's version of the 'Coronation Scot'. No. 4489 did not achieve speeds as high as No. 6220 had done the day before, its train was 50 tons heavier, 320 tons as compared to 270 – and no crockery was smashed.

Furthermore, any serious comparisons had to take into account the fact that the first 150 miles of the East Coast Main Line out of London is steeper that the west coast counterpart, with sizeable 1-in-200 stretches.

Yet *Dominion of Canada* did not do badly at all, hitting 109.5mph while descending Stoke Bank. Indeed, while No. 6220 had been driven at speeds higher than were intended for the new LMS streamlined train, No. 4489 was travelling just above the expected speed for the route.

On July 12, 1937, two weeks after the record run, Tom Clark was rostered to take charge of the Royal Train on a journey from Edinburgh to Euston. When it arrived at Euston, Sir Josiah Stamp, approached the footplate and said: "Come on, Tom, the King has something for you."

Still wearing the overalls in which he had driven the train, Tom walked to the King's coach. There, King George VI, who had been travelling with Queen Elizabeth, Princess Elizabeth and Princess Margaret, presented him with the OBE awarded to him in the Coronation Honours List, together with royal congratulations on his record-breaking run with No. 6201 the year before.

On August 304 1937, No. 6221 *Queen Elizabeth* worked the Royal Train from Euston

This Lancashire & Yorkshire Railway dynamometer car was used to test locomotives such as the Royal Scot, Princess Royal and Coronation classes. Built in 1912 and original numbered 293, after the Grouping it became LMS No. 45050. Withdrawn in 1967, it is now preserved. ROBIN JONES

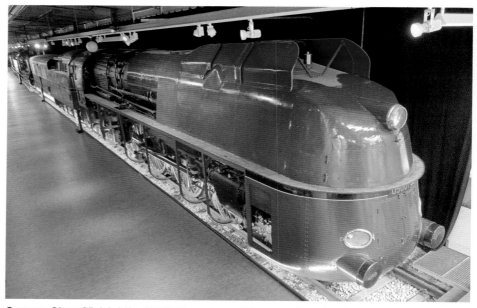

German Class 05 4-6-4 No. 05001, the sole surviving member of a class of three which once included No. 05002, which on May 11, 1936, set a new world steam speed record of 124.5mph. It is displayed inside Nuremberg's Deutsche Bahn Museum. ROBIN JONES

to Carlisle, where it handed over to 4-4-0 compounds Nos. 1147 and 1149 to take the train onwards to Perth.

However, by then the fate of the crockery at Crewe led to the rivals agreeing to call a halt to risky record-breaking trips which had been staged for public relations purpose.

Tom Clark retired in 1938 and continued to live in Crewe, passing his time fishing and playing snooker.

He died after a short illness in January

1954, at the age of 80, by which time he had inspired a generation or two or three.

History records that it would be the LNER that did, however, have the final word on steam, not just in this race to the north, but for all time.

In response the German 124.5mph in 1936, and then to Clark's allegedly 114mph feat with *Coronation*, A4 No. 4468 *Mallard* set an all-time world steam locomotive record near Lttle Bytham on Stoke Bank on July 3, 1938.

Wax figures recreate a typical test run scene inside restored dynamometer car No. 45050 at the Princess Royal Class Locomotive Trust's West Shed home, the base of preserved No. 6233 *Duchess of Sutherland*, at the Midland Railway – Butterley.

A dynamometer car is attached behind a locomotive and measures its performance by means of a drawbar attached to a nest of horizontally placed springs beneath the floor which deflect under load.

An arm connected to the springs comes up through the floor and transmits the deflection up to the recording table, allowing it to be used to calculate the horsepower generated by means of a mechanical integrator mounted on the table. The output was then automatically recorded by means of one of several pens making traces on a moving roll of paper drawn under them at a known rate. Needless to say, GPS was not available in Stanier and Gresley's days.

An independent road wheel with a diameter of 33.613in is located between the bogie wheels near to the observation end of the car. This wheel can be lowered onto the track and used to drive all of the elements of the instrument table which depend on the running speed and recording distance travelled.

Other information such as water and coal consumption are marked on the dynamometer car roll during tests.

By means of visual observation by engineers seated high up in the 'balloon' end of the car, next to the tender, each shovel of coal delivered into the firebox can be recorded, while the consumption of water is measured by a pre-calibrated U-tube gauge. Events were recorded by using a bell push and a system of bell codes and marked as such on the moving roll of paper.

This vehicle played a role in the 1948 Locomotive Exchange Trials to evaluate various locomotive types used by the 'Big Four' companies, compiling data which was used in the design of the British Railways Standard classes, which it also tested.

In 1948 it tested the first main line diesel electric locomotives used on Britain's railways, Nos. 10000 and 10001. ROBIN JONES

Driver Joe Duddington, a man renowned like Tom Clark for driving at speed, and fireman Tom Bray were chosen for the journey from Barkston Junction north of Grantham back to King's Cross, which had been arranged ostensibly for the trials of a new quick acting Westinghouse QSA brake.

The big end bearing of *Mallard*'s middle cylinder overheated on the record run, and at Peterborough, No. 4468 had to be taken off the trip for repairs. Nonetheless, Gresley had taken the record, not just from Stanier's finest, but from Nazi Germany.

There would be no further speed records by British locomotives. Gresley wanted to try for 130mph with an A4, but the Second World War precluded any such attempts, when maximum speeds were imposed because of the heavy loadings on trains.

After the war, track maintenance arrears had built up, and the permanent way was not considered sufficiently safe for racing trains.

It would be only in the diesel and electric era that *Mallard*'s record would be surpassed. ■

On September 7-8, 2013 in a hugely successful local event sponsored by *The Railway Magazine*, No. 4468 *Mallard* returned to Grantham station, through which it had sped 75 years earlier, on Sunday, July 3, 1938, before setting the all-time world steam railway locomotive speed record at Little Bytham on Stoke bank. ROBIN JONES

CHAPTER FOUR

FROM BLUE AND RED TO BLACK: THE STREAMLINE ERA

Colour pictures of blue and silver Princess Coronation Pacifics in action are rare. No. 6222 *Queen Mary*, outshopped from Crewe on June 22, 1937, is seen leaving Euston with the Down 'Coronation Scot' in the summer of 1938. When withdrawn on October 26, 1963, *Queen Mary* had the lowest annual mileage – 55,723 – of any class member. Only its regulator handle is preserved – fitted to No. 6229 *Duchess of Hamilton*. HL OVEREND/COLOUR-RAIL LM65

Inaugurated in 1937 for the coronation of George VI, and a classic product of the zenith of the steam era, the 'Coronation Scot' ran from Euston to Glasgow Central for just three years, from 1937 until the outbreak of the Second World War.

Intended to compete with the rival East Coast Main Line services, the 'Coronation Scot' was scheduled to complete the journey from London to Glasgow in six hours 30 minutes. The scheduled time over the 299 miles from Euston to Carlisle was four hours 43 minutes, an average speed of 63.4mph.

It stopped only at Carlisle to change the locomotive crew and to pick up and set down passengers to and from London.

In the summer of 1937, the 'Coronation Scot' was the longest run in the world scheduled at more than 60mph.

Behind the glamorous Pacific heading the train was a rake of matching coaches, air-conditioned and soundproofed. They comprised existing LMS carriages that had been also painted in Caledonian Railway blue livery. The image of the train epitomised a great age of post-slump optimism that would soon be sharply brought to an end.

Composer Eric Coates produced a popular piece of music called Coronation Scot: however, he wrote it while sitting in the Great

Princess Coronation Pacific No. 6224 *Princess Alexandra*, the last of the blue streamliners, at Shrewsbury in 1938. Withdrawn in October 19, 1963, it had 11 boiler changes in its career, more than any other member of the class. P WHITEHOUSE/COLOUR-RAIL LM20

Western's 'Cornish Riviera Express'.

Stanier's masterpiece had shown itself to be an instant success, and orders were placed at Crewe Works for the construction of 10 more locomotives, Nos. 6225-6234, each of which carried the name of a duchess (No. 6225 *Gloucester*, No. 6226 *Norfolk*, No. 6227 *Devonshire*, No. 6228 *Rutland*, No. 6229

Hamilton, No. 6230 *Buccleuch*, No. 6231 *Atholl*, No. 6232 *Montrose*, No. 6233 *Sutherland*, No. 6234 *Abercorn*). The term duchess quickly became commonly used to describe the whole class.

Nos. 6225-9 were streamlined, but 6230-4 were not. Neither were the latter engines initially fitted with the smoke deflectors at that time which gave the class their familiar appearance in

LMS

CREWE WORKS
BUILDING "CORONATION" CLASS ENGINES

LMS poster from 1937 depicting the building of a Princess Coronation Pacific in Crewe Works. NRM

The prestigious LMS 'Coronation Scot' streamlined service headed by No. 6222 *Queen Mary* heads through Shap from Euston to Glasgow on July 24, 1939. MAURICE EARLEY/NRM

the British Railways' era. These 10 were outshopped between May and August 1938.

The second batch of streamlined locomotives, Nos. 6225-6229, were painted in crimson lake, with banding in gold lined with vermilion and black. The nameplates had a black background. LMS works grey was carried briefly in service on *Duchess of Hamilton* from September 7, 1938 until its return to Crewe Works later that year on December 8, to be painted crimson lake.

Nos. 6230-6234 were painted in a special version of the LMS standard crimson lake

livery – the locomotives were lined out in gold, bordered with fine red lines, with serif lettering and numerals in gold leaf and vermilion shading. Handrails and sundry small external fittings were chrome-plated, as were the nameplates, which had a black background.

Trials with No. 6234 *Duchess of Abercorn* hauling a 600-ton train between Crewe and Glasgow were undertaken in 1939. The first took place on February 12 and the second on February 26, in between which No. 6234 was equipped with a double chimney. The second

trial resulted in what is believed to be a record horsepower output for a British steam engine of 3333hp.

The late LMS authority David Jenkinson wrote in *Heritage Railway* magazine in 2001, that in terms of absolute power: "The Duchess type stood supreme and was never bettered."

He wrote: "What, therefore, do I mean by power? Well, it has nothing to do with quoted nominal tractive effort, purely mathematical calculation based on cylinder size, boiler pressure and wheel diameter, paying no attention to efficiency.

No. 6221 *Queen Elizabeth* hauling the 'Coronation Scot' up Camden Bank, with Jubilee 4-6-0 No. 5563 *Australia* backing up towards Camden shed, on September 23, 1938. No. 6221, which came out of Crewe Works on June 14, 1937, four years later became the only blue streamliner to be repainted crimson lake, and was also unique in that it was the only member of the class ever to be equipped with a Princess Royal-type tender without the coal pusher, two years before it was withdrawn on May 18, 1963. NRM

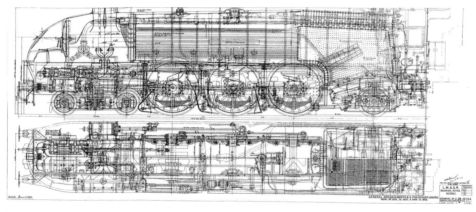

The LMS drawings for the Princess Coronation Pacific class. LMS

"On this basis, there were a number of British designs which could quote an equal or superior figure to the Stanier design. In fact, a true appraisal of power is entirely to do with what is left to pull the train after the engine has moved itself and its tender, a matter of 160 tons or so (equal to about five coaches) in the case of the Duchesses and most large 4-6-2s. It is called drawbar horsepower and how much is left over for the train itself is usually a measure of how efficiently the steam has been used between generation in the boiler and final exhaust to atmosphere.

"In most cases, horsepower is quoted in two versions, 'indicated horsepower' (ihp – produced in the cylinders before any work is done) and 'drawbar horsepower' (dhp – produced, as its name suggests, at the back of the tender and available to pull the train).

"These figures can be either measured or calculated and it is on record that the Stanier Duchess stands supreme on both counts as a result of trials made with No. 6234 *Duchess of Abercorn* before the war (which led to the fitting of double chimneys) and No. 46225 *Duchess of Gloucester* in early BR days, including some monumentally prodigious efforts over the Settle and Carlisle route.

"Even before the war, a Stanier Duchess had produced more horsepower in its cylinders than even the celebrated Deltics could achieve a generation later.

"I therefore consider that as far as sheer power is concerned, the Duchesses were never equalled and probably never put to the ultimate test on the road."

More streamlined members of the class were built, with Nos. 6235-9 appearing in July-September 1939. The war initially interrupted the building of further locomotives, but given the dire shortage of express motive power, several more were then completed, Nos. 6236-

Non-streamlined No. 6232 *Duchess of Montrose* at Shrewsbury in 1938. No. 6232 was the third of the non-streamliners, outshopped from Crewe on July 1, 1938. It was damaged in a Luftwaffe bombing raid in 1940. When withdrawn on December 29, 1962, it was the only class member still with its original boiler. P WHITEHOUSE/COLOUR-RAIL LM21

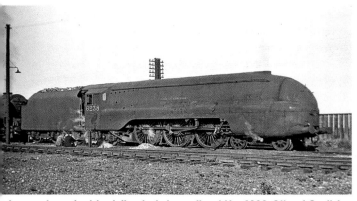

A rare view of a black-liveried streamlined No. 6238 *City of Carlisle*, the first Princess Coronation Pacific built during the Second World War, illustrating the less-than-complimentary description of the design as an 'upside down jelly mould'. P HUGHES/COLOUR-RAIL 95375

No. 6220 *Coronation* and the 'Coronation Scot' train with a replica of Stephenson's *Rocket* on display at Crewe Works on May 25, 1937. NRM

44 between March and July 1940 and Nos. 6245-48 from June to October 1943.

Nos. 6235-6244 were painted in crimson lake with gold stripes and black borders.

While single chimneys initially fitted to Nos. 6220-6234 when built, they were replaced with double chimneys between 1939 and 1944. From No. 6235 onwards, class members were built with double chimneys.

Streamliners Nos. 6245-6248 were outshopped at Crewe in 1943 in plain wartime unlined black livery as an austerity measure. The following batch, Nos. 6249-6252, were outshopped minus streamlined fairings, but with streamlined tenders, and again painted unlined black with red-shaded yellow numerals and lettering.

The final wartime build was of non-streamlined Nos. 6249-52 between April and June 1944. Nos. 6235-52 were all named after cities, but No. 6244 City of Leeds was renamed *King George VI* in April 1941, with *City of Leeds* reappearing on No. 6248. In March 1946 No. 6234 *Duchess of Abercorn* was painted in a blue/grey colour, a proposed new postwar livery, one version of which had a pale straw yellow line along the running plate, yellow and black edging to cab and tender, and unshaded numerals and lettering.

The production of the class continued after the war, with the names of Nos. 6253-5 continuing the city theme.

IVATT'S DUCHESSES

In 1942, Stanier began a full-time secondment to the Ministry of Production. He was knighted on February 9, 1943 for services to railways and the country. He retired in 1944, and was elected a Fellow of the Royal Society. Also in 1944, he became president of the Institution of Mechanical Engineers.

Appointed in his place as acting chief mechanical engineer in 1942 was Charles Fairburn, whose railway career began in 1912 at the Siemens Brothers dynamo works in Stafford, where he worked in the railway engineering department.

He joined the LMS in 1934 as chief electrical engineer, and four years later was appointed deputy chief mechanical engineer. He was responsible for the introduction of diesel-electric shunters on the LMS, paving the way for British Railways' mass dieselisation.

Princess Coronation Pacifics Nos. No 6224 *Princess Alexandra* and No. 6230 *Duchess of Buccleuch* among the locomotives being prepared at Camden shed, as portrayed in an LMS souvenir booklet produced to mark 1938's 100th anniversary of the London & Birmingham Railway. ROBIN JONES COLLECTION

A quintessential art deco era poster: the 'Coronation Scot' ascends Shap Fell. LMS/NRM

Princess Coronation Pacific No. 6221 *Queen Elizabeth* leaving Edinburgh Princes Street with a service to Glasgow in 1938. To the right stands a Caledonian Railway 0-4-4T.
P RANSOME WALLIS / *THE RAILWAY MAGAZINE*

William Stanier at work in his office: a waxwork at the Princess Royal Class Locomotive Trust's West Shed base at the Midland Railway-Butterley. ROBIN JONES

No. 6221 *Queen Elizabeth* heads the Down 'Coronation Scot' up Shap. MAURICE EARLEY / *THE RAILWAY MAGAZINE*

In 1938, the LMS held an exhibition at Euston to mark the centenary of the London & Birmingham Railway. Exhibition locomotives returning from Euston to Camden are No. 6225 *Duchess of Gloucester*, LNWR George the Fifth 4-4-0 No. 25348 *Coronation*, LNWR 2-2-2 No. 3020 *Cornwall*, and a Jubilee 4-6-0. No. 6225 was the first Princess Coronation Pacific to be titled 'Duchess' and also the first to be painted from new in LMS crimson lake. In 1955, No. 6225 underwent tests at the Rugby testing plant which established the claim of the class to be the "most powerful". The LMS and rival LNER agreed in 1937 to build the plant, but it was not completed until 1948. Emerging from Crewe on May 11, 1938, No. 6225 was withdrawn on September 12, 1964. ER WETHERINGSETT/*THE RAILWAY MAGAZINE*

On Stanier's retirement, he was appointed CME. However, he died from a heart attack on October 12, 1945, aged 58, so the job was given to Henry George Ivatt, the last chief mechanical engineer of the LMS. The son of Great Northern Railway locomotive engineer Henry Ivatt, he started his railway career as an LNWR apprentice at Crewe in 1904.

He worked his way up to the post of assistant foreman at Crewe North Shed in 1909, and during the First World War Ivatt served on the staff of the director of transport in France. In 1919, he became assistant locomotive superintendent of the North Staffordshire Railway, which became part of the LMS at the Grouping.

Appointed Derby Locomotive Works superintendent in 1931, the following year Ivatt was made divisional mechanical engineer, Scotland. In 1937, he became principal assistant for locomotives to Stanier.

Ivatt modified the design of the Princess Coronations. The last two members of the class appeared with a redesigned rear frame, a cast steel trailing truck and roller bearings on all axles. The pair were instantly recognisable

Outshopped from Crewe on June 26, 1943, the year in which the works celebrated its centenary, No. 6245 *City of London* was the first streamliner painted in wartime unlined black, with lettering and numbers in red-shaded yellow. In its rebuilt form, in 1957, it became the first Duchess to be painted in British Railways' maroon, but with LMS-style lining and never the BR pattern. Withdrawn on September 12, 1964, ironically it was one of the last three Duchesses to be based in London. *THE RAILWAY MAGAZINE*

Princess Coronation Pacific No. 6223 *Princess Alice* hauls the 'Coronation Scot' at speed. Outshopped from Crewe on June 28, 1937, it was withdrawn by British Railways in 1963.
THE RAILWAY MAGAZINE

The appearance of the glamorous Princess Coronation Pacifics sparked off the production of souvenir merchandise, especially for younger fans! ROBIN JONES

by the squared-off cab bottom.

No. 6256 emerged from Crewe in December 1946 in lined black livery. It was the last express passenger engine built by the LMS and was named *Sir William A. Stanier F.R.S.* in honour of its designer.

The last Princess Coronation of all was built by British Railways. *City of Salford* emerged from Crewe Works in May 1948 and, with the prefix 4 added to the class numbers, was No. 46257 from the outset.

THE END OF THE STREAMLINERS

Smoke deflectors were added from 1945, while the last five locomotives had smoke deflectors fitted from new.

Changes to the class in later times saw the adding of smoke deflectors to the non-streamlined versions after claims that drifting smoke obscured the crew's forward vision, a matter often debated by experts.

The first to be fitted with smoke deflectors was No. 6252 *City of Leicester* in March 1945 and the last No. 46243 *City of Lancaster* in May 1949, while Nos. 6253-6 and 46257 had them from new.

The fitting of the deflectors coincided in many cases with the removal of the streamlining, which started in April 1946 with No. 6235 *City of Birmingham* and finished with No. 46243 in May 1949.

The naming of No. 6245 *City of London* took place at Euston on July 20, 1943. From left are LMS chairman Sir Thomas Royden, the Lady Mayoress, and the Lord Mayor of London, Sir Samuel G Joseph. *THE RAILWAY MAGAZINE*

The penultimate Princess Coronation to be built, No. 6256, also the 50th LMS Pacific, emerged from Crewe Works on December 13, 1947. Stanier was brought back out of retirement to officially name it Sir William A. Stanier F.R.S. The initials FRS stand for Fellow of the Royal Society: in 1944, Stanier became the only railway engineer apart from George Stephenson to receive that accolade. One of the last two Duchesses built with Ivatt's modifications so they could be compared with the new LMS main line diesel designs, it was withdrawn on October 3, 1964. PRCLT

The great days of glamorous fast luxury expresses belonged to the 1930s, and in the postwar era, streamlined cases were not only seen as an anachronism but impeded maintenance, restricting access to parts which needed daily attention. Some of the casings looked increasingly shabby as depots removed bits of them here and there to improve access to the working parts, and never replaced them.

The matt black livery did nothing for the railway in terms of prestige, especially when the casings became caked with grime, and with trains both in wartime and the postwar era limited to 75mph, there seemed no purpose in retaining the streamlining, when what lay below was more than good enough.

The destreamlined locomotives were instantly recognisable to railwaymen and enthusiasts because the top of the smokebox retained the slope that had been required to accommodate the bulbous front-end design.

New boilers or rebuilt smokeboxes gradually saw this feature disappear during the 1950s but it was not until May 1960 that it was eliminated with No. 46246 *City of Manchester* being the last incumbent.

The class members which were not streamlined were by then referred to outright as Duchesses, while those which retained the smokebox from the streamlined era were called 'semis'. ∎

A wartime black-liveried Princess Coronation Pacific passes Tring in 1944. *THE RAILWAY MAGAZINE*

CHAPTER FIVE

A PRINCESS CORONATION
TAKES THE STATES BY STORM

We have seen that No. 6229 *Duchess of Hamilton* did not initially appear in crimson lake livery when it emerged from Crewe Works on September 7, 1938.

Instead, it ran in grey works undercoat for three months until it returned to Crewe Works

to be painted in LMS crimson lake livery. There was a reason. It was to exchange identities with No. 6220 *Coronation* – and, along with a complete 'Coronation Scot' train, represent the LMS at no less than the New York World's Fair in 1939-40.

This event was the second largest American world's fair of all time, exceeded only by the Louisiana Purchase Exposition of 1904 in St Louis. Many countries around the world took part, and more than 44 million

people attended over its two seasons. The fair site covered 1216 acres of Flushing Meadows and Corona Park. The central theme was the future, with an opening slogan of "Dawn of a New Day", and it set out to showcase "the world of tomorrow".

The official New York World's Fair pamphlet said: "The eyes of the fair are on the future – not in the sense of peering toward the unknown nor attempting to foretell the events of tomorrow and the shape of things to come,

Resplendent in the LMS crimson lake that the real No. 6220 *Coronation* never carried, Princess Coronation Pacific No. 6229 *Duchess of Hamilton* stands at the head of its 'Coronation Scot' train at the 1939 New York World's Fair.
COLOUR-RAIL LM102

but in the sense of presenting a new and clearer view of today in preparation for tomorrow; a view of the forces and ideas that prevail as well as the machines.

"To its visitors the fair will say: 'Here are the materials, ideas, and forces at work in our world. These are the tools with which the World of Tomorrow must be made. They are all interesting and much effort has been expended to lay them before you in an interesting way. Familiarity with today is the best preparation for the future.'"

By this time, Sir Josiah Stamp, the man who headhunted William Stanier from the GWR, had become Lord Stamp. He was raised to the peerage on June 28, 1938, as Baron Stamp of

Shortlands in Kent. A special brochure was produced by the LMS to mark the visit of 'No. 6220' to the USA, In it, as chairman and president of the LMS executive, he wrote: "Why are we sending the Coronation Scot train to America?

"In 1933 we sent you an ambassador of goodwill and technical achievement, the 'Royal Scot' train. You responded magnificently and the train was crowded wherever it stopped, from morn till night. Millions went miles just to watch her go by. New as tomorrow, it yet made thousands feel a touch with the Old Country.

"The 'Royal Scot' made many friends for Great Britain, for those officers of my company who were associated with the venture, and for myself.

"The 'Coronation Scot', which comes to you as the latest product of the science of British railroading, comes then as a cementer of these friendships. It will make a tour of the United States, be our exhibit at the World's Fair in

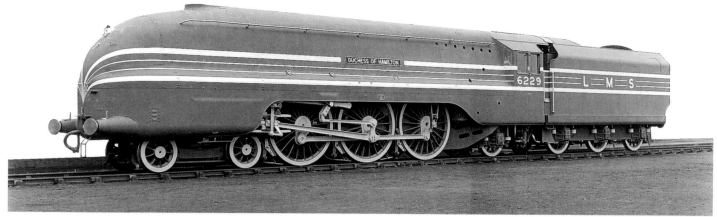

Duchess of Hamilton at Crewe Works on May 26, 1938. NRM

The bell and light installed on No. 6229 in preparation for its journey to the 1939 New York World's Fair. NRM

The 'Coronation Scot' brochure for the 1939 New York World's Fair.

New York, where we of the LMS feel that we are providing a representative worthy of this important occasion. We believe, too, that the 'Coronation Scot' provides visible evidence of the advance that has been made in Great Britain in railroad transportation since the 'Royal Scot' visited you six years ago.

"May we also hope that the visit of the 'Coronation Scot' can have an even wider significance than mere commercial objects? There is nobody in Great Britain who does not admire the courage and foresight shown in organising the New York World's Fair at a time when trade has been receding and when the world outlook is not wholly peaceful. Yet, just as in 1933 the visit of the 'Royal Scot' preceded a revival in business and industrial activity on both sides of the Atlantic, so may we hope the World's Fair and this new tour of an LMS train will coincide with a new period of peace and prosperity for both our nations."

THE SPECIAL STEAM RELATIONSHIP

There has always been a special relationship between the USA and Britain, at least in the

Crowds flock to welcome 'No. 6220 *Coronation*' to Hartford, Connecticut. *THE RAILWAY MAGAZINE*

world of railways, from the earliest days of steam. It was Britain that supplied the first steam locomotives to the US.

The Delaware and Hudson Canal Company sent its chief engineer Horatio Allen to England in 1826, and he ordered a locomotive from Robert Stephenson. He then visited Stourbridge, where Foster & Rastrick had its Bradley Iron Works.

Partner John Urpeth Rastrick had worked with John Trevithick in Cornwall, and also knew Robert Stephenson. Allen ordered three locomotives from the firm.

Stephenson's locomotive, *Pride of Newcastle*, was delivered across the Atlantic first, two months before the Stourbridge three. However, the locomotive chosen for the trials on August 8, 1828, was Foster & Rastrick's 0-4-0 *Stourbridge Lion*, possibly because at 7.5 tons it was the lightest, and the canal company's plans for a railroad involved rails made of wood.

A huge crowd gathered at Honesdale, Pennsylvania, to watch the locomotive become the first to steam in the USA. The *Stourbridge Lion*, similar to *Agenoria* which is displayed in the National Railway Museum at York, was recorded in 1834 as being retired.

Britain continued to export locomotives to early US railroads.

Built by Robert Stephenson & Company, 0-4-0 No. 1 *John Bull* was exported to the Camden & Amboy Railroad, the first railroad in New Jersey, and operated for the first time on September 15, 1831. It became the oldest operable steam locomotive in the world when the Smithsonian Institution ran it in 1981.

Princess Coronation Pacific No. 6229 *Duchess of Hamilton* as No. 6220 *Coronation* departs Hartford, Connecticut, on the New York, New Haven & Hartford Railroad during its US tour. *THE RAILWAY MAGAZINE*

In 1893, the World's Columbian Exposition, also known as The Chicago World's Fair, marked the 400th anniversary of Christopher Columbus's arrival in the New World in 1492.

The fair covered over 600 acres and was attended by more than 27 million people over its six month run. With more than 200 temporary neoclassical buildings erected, in terms of scale and grandeur it far exceeded other world fairs, and became to the US what the Great Exhibition of 1851 in Crystal Palace had been to the UK.

Two British locomotives attended. The GWR sent Iron Duke 4-2-2 *Lord of the Isles*, which had been shown at the Great Exhibition in London after being built the same year. Ironically, it was displayed as a prime

example of British engineering excellence, which the Iron Duke class members were – in their day – more than a year after Brunel's 7ft 0¼in broad gauge had finally been eradicated on the GWR.

The other British exhibit at the 1893 fair was a complete train, sent by the LNWR, comprising three-cylinder compound 2-4-2 (or, more accurately, 2-2-2-2) No. 2054 *Queen Empress*, known by the footplate staff as the Scarlet Runner, and a pair of coaches.

LNWR director Miles MacInnes visited the fair during site construction and noted that it was "on such a scale that St Pancras railway station would stand in a corner without being much noticed and the speed at which the work is going on is marvellous".

Two GWR locomotives crossed the ocean in 1927 to attend the Fair of the Iron Horse in Baltimore, Maryland, the centenary celebrations for the Baltimore & Ohio Railroad, one of the oldest railroads in the US and the first common carrier railroad. Among the extensive locomotive line-up was none other than *John Bull*.

Another world's fair took place in Chicago during 1933-34 to mark the city's centenary. The theme of the fair, A Century of Progress International Exposition, was technological innovation, with the motto 'Science finds, industry applies, man adapts'. As Lord Stamp reminded everyone in his tour brochure

King George VI and Queen Elizabeth visit the Canadian Pavilion at the World's Fair.

foreword, the LMS sent No. 6100 *Royal Scot* and a matching rake of typical LMS coaches.

In reality, however, the locomotive was not the original No. 6100, but No. 6152 *The King's Dragoon Guardsman*, which had been built at Derby in 1930 and which was considered a better performer. The pair exchanged identities for the fair and kept them afterwards.

No. 6100 toured both the US and Canada, covering 11,194 miles and being inspected by more than three million people. As happened with *King George V*, it was given special commemorative plates.

BLUE TURNS TO RED

So in 1939 the LMS decided to venture once more across the Atlantic to exhibit its most modern train to the rest of the world.

The eight carriages accompanying the impostor 'Coronation' were built in Derby. The train comprised three articulated pairs of coaches, a sleeping car and a club car.

The identity exchange left a blue-liveried 'No. 6229 *Duchess of Hamilton*' running in Britain, and a crimson lake 'Coronation' in North America, when the true colours were the other way round.

The locomotive crew selected to make the trip 'across the pond' comprised driver Fred C Bishop and passed fireman John Carswell, both of

Camden shed. The pair had been presented with watches by King Boris of Bulgaria when he rode on the real *Coronation's* footplate with them.

Senior Crewe Works foreman F W Soden was placed in charge of maintenance, while Stanier's principal assistant Robert Riddles took overall charge of the trip.

To comply with US railroad laws, No. 6229/6220 was fitted with a huge headlamp and brass bell along with brackets for side lamps and a claw coupling. None of the other LMS streamliners ever had such features.

The tour train ran from Crewe to Euston where it was publicly unveiled on January 9, 1939, with the LMS publicity machine shaking a ripe apple tree.

The footplate crew gave a TV interview at Alexandra Palace and then Lord Stamp presided over a farewell lunch at the Euston Hotel.

The train including 'Coronation' was hauled from Willesden to Southampton Docks and loaded aboard the Norwegian MV Belpamela which was specially designed for shipping railway vehicles. The Southern Railway laid a temporary track to its new Ocean Quay before the 'Coronation Scot' arrived to be loaded. Several components of the Princess Coronation were packed separately. The ship finally sailed on January 26, with Riddles

Crowds gather to inspect the 'Coronation Scot' at Washington's Union station. NRM

Returning from Washington DC to Baltimore on its March 18, 1939, press trip, the 'Coronation Scot' was stopped on the Thomas Viaduct over the Patusco River near Relay, Maryland. Built in 1835, it is said to be the world's oldest stone railway viaduct. 'Coronation' was posed for press pictures alongside the Baltimore & Ohio Railroad's 'Capitol Limited' headed by streamlined P7 Pacific No. 5304.

The interior of the 'Coronation Scot' train exhibited at Euston in January 1939 before its shipment to America. *NRM*

taking a berth on the *Queen Mary* and his crew following behind on the *Aquitania*. They arrived in the States before the Belpamela, where bad weather had made it six days later arriving in Baltimore on February 20.

The train was unloaded four days later, and taken to the Baltimore & Ohio Railroad's workshops at Mount Clare for the locomotive to be reassembled.

STEAMING STATESIDE

A private test run was followed by an unveiling to a VIP audience in the workshops on March 17, with a press run to Washington and back the next day.

The train first made a 3121 mile tour of the US, hosted by the Baltimore & Ohio Railroad, as a build-up to the World's Fair. It began on March 21, with the starting signal being electrically activated directly from the fairground. The firebox brick arch looked set to collapse three days later, and had to be

No. 6229 disguised as No. 6220 *Coronation* leaves Washington DC during its 1939 tour. *NRM*

Among the many ground-breaking locomotives on display along with 'No. 6220 *Coronation*' in the World's Fair Transportation Zone was the Pennsylvania Railroad's unique S1 experimental locomotive mounted on rollers under the driver wheels and running continuously at 60mph all day long. The S1 was the only locomotive ever built with a 6-4-4-6 wheel arrangement. It was a duplex locomotive, meaning that it had two pairs of cylinders, each driving two pairs of driving wheels, and also the longest and heaviest rigid frame reciprocating steam locomotive ever built. Completed on January 31, 1939, and numbered 6100, it was found to be too big for many curves and suffered from wheel slippage. Its last run was in December 1945 and it was scrapped in 1949.

replaced before the daunting climb through the Allegheny Mountains was tackled.

The tour was a rip-roaring success, 'Coronation' attracting crowds wherever it went. It was estimated that around 425,000 came on board at the stations to inspect the luxurious interior. That was small beer compared to the two million people who viewed it at the fair itself.

The grand opening of the fair took place on Sunday, April 30, the 150th anniversary of George Washington's inauguration as president in New York City. Around 206,000 people attended, even though many of the pavilions and other facilities were not ready.

David Sarnoff, president of RCA, displayed a TV set at the opening for the world to see. Before the fair, the firm had published a brochure for its dealers to explain television.

As a reflection of the wide range of technological innovation on parade at the fair, Franklin D Roosevelt's speech was televised along with other parts of the opening ceremony and other events at the fair. Roosevelt was seen on black and white television sets with 5in tubes.

NBC used the event to inaugurate regularly scheduled television broadcasts in New York City, and an estimated 1000 people viewed the president's broadcast on about 200 television sets throughout the New York area. After this formal introduction of television sets, they became widely available for the public.

Albert Einstein gave a speech which discussed cosmic rays before the ceremonial lighting of the fair's lights.

That May, Riddles came home expecting to go back later that year to bring the train home. It did not happen as planned. The outbreak of war in September 1939 led to shipping cargoes being restricted to food and military supplies.

The World's Fair organisers asked for 'Coronation' to be exhibited for another year. The LMS had no alternative but to agree.

The 'Coronation Scot' train at Jefferson, Indiana, where it was stationed as living quarters for officers of the USA Army Quartermaster Corps. *THE RAILWAY MAGAZINE*

The interior of the 'Coronation Scot' train used as army living quarters, as pictured in 1943. *THE RAILWAY MAGAZINE*

AN EXILE RETURNS

However, despite the shipping losses that were being incurred during the German U-boat offensive in the Atlantic, by 1942 the LMS – hit by a shortage of locomotives – wanted No. 6229 back.

It was considered that the need for No. 6229 outweighed the risk of seeing it end up at the bottom of the Atlantic in the hold of a torpedoed ship.

So it was taken from the Mount Clare workshops where it had been stored and loaded on to the *SS Pioneer*.

To the relief of all concerned, it arrived back safely at Queen Alexandra Dock in Cardiff on February 16, 1942, and was then hauled via Hereford and Shrewsbury to Crewe.

It re-entered service as No. 6220 *Coronation*, minus the US headlamp and bell. Only a year later did it revert to being No. 6229 *Duchess of Hamilton* again, when both engines were in for repair at Crewe.

Back in its rightful identity, it remained at Crewe North shed until the end of the year before being transferred to Camden, where it stayed until 1947.

The carriages did not accompany the locomotive back home however. After the fair closed, they were loaned to the US Army Quartermaster Corps as officer living accommodation.

The carriages finally came back in 1946, but by then the 'Coronation Scot' was no more.

The three sets of nine blue/silver striped 'Coronation Scot coaches reappeared in 1947 repainted in plain red, but never went back as three sets of nine coaches running the famous named train ever again.

Only one 'Coronation Scot' vehicle survives; 1936-built Restaurant Corridor Kitchen Car (later rebuilt as a British Railways Inspection Saloon) No. 30088 (later TDM395279) from the third blue set eventually became a holiday home at privately owned Rowden Mill station

in Herefordshire. It was then moved to Titley Junction station in Herefordshire, where a private standard gauge railway has been laid, and converted again to holiday accommodation as 'The Coronation Scot Sleeper'. Painted red, it bears little resemblance to its catering days on the streamliner service.

MAKING FRIENDS OF FOES

Sadly, in his foreword to the 'Coronation Scot' tour brochure, Lord Stamp was spot on when he wrote that "the world outlook is not wholly peaceful".

Surprising, therefore, that he was lulled into a false sense of hope by Prime Minister Neville Chamberlain's "peace in our time" that there would never be another world war, and agreed to allow the 'Coronation Ascot' to visit the US, turning a deaf ear to those like Winston Churchill who were predicting dire consequences in the times ahead.

At the age of 60, Lord Stamp refused to be moved out of his home, Tantallon, in Park Hill Road, Shortlands, because of Luftwaffe bombing during the Blitz.

He, along with his wife, aged 63, and their son Wilfred died as a result of a direct hit on the air raid shelter at their home on April 16, 1941.

There was more than a touch of irony here, because in 1935 he had become a founder member of the Anglo-German Fellowship. As such, he made a low-key visit to Nuremberg the following year and met none other than Adolf Hitler, who he described as a "statesman and demagogue combined". He returned in 1937 to view the Nazi Party Congress, with the unspoken support of Foreign Secretary Lord Halifax.

LIFE BACK HOME

No. 6229 *Duchess of Hamilton* was painted into wartime unlined black livery in November 1944. Its streamlined casing was removed in December 1947 for maintenance-efficiency reasons and it was then given the LMS 1946 black livery. In 1948 it passed into British Railways ownership, with 40000 added to its number to become No. 46229 on April 15 that year.

In April 1950, *Duchess of Hamilton* was painted in the short-lived BR express passenger blue livery, On April 26, 1952, it was changed into Brunswick green.

The semi-streamlined smokebox was replaced with a round-topped version in February 1957, and in September 1958, No. 46229 was painted maroon. ■

CHAPTER SIX

THE DAY OF THE DUCHESSES

The first of the class, No. 46220 *Coronation*, in its rebuilt form and carrying British Railways' Brunswick green livery, at Euston in 1961. Withdrawn on April 20, 1963, after getting through seven boilers and five tenders, the question will always be asked – why was it not preserved? COLOUR-RAIL BRM13

William Stanier and his team had designed the Princess Coronation class not only with raw power but style and prestige uppermost in their thoughts. A locomotive capable of 3300hp was the complete antitheses of the Midland Railway small-engine policy which had been banished to the past.

However, the rebuilding of the class into non-streamlined versions, stripping away the art deco streamlined casings, saw the class lose none of their power and certainly none of their appeal.

During steam's 'Indian summer' of the 1950s, they built up an enormous following in the enthusiast fraternity, members of which were wowed by their traditional locomotive appearance.

From new until the end of the Fifties, the class covered all the front line expresses on the West Coast Main Line, which meant that they could be seen anywhere between Euston

ABOVE: Resplendent in British Railways' maroon livery, rebuilt No. 46226 *Duchess of Norfolk* heads out of the 2432 yard Kilsby tunnel on the West Coast Main Line in Northamptonshire in September 1960. Outshopped on May 23, 1938, it was withdrawn on September 12, 1964, one of the last in service.
COLOUR-RAIL BRM2255

Carlisle Citadel station in the mid-Fifties: rebuilt No. 46244 *King George VI* heads the Euston to Glasgow 'Royal Scot' while sister engine No. 46231 *Duchess of Atholl* took over for the journey north. No. 6244 was the last of the red streamliners, and was originally called *City of Leeds*, only to be renamed for patriotic reasons in 1941. It often worked the Royal Train.

King George VI laid claim to the fastest postwar long-distance Duchess performance when it took the 'Caledonian' 299 miles from Carlisle to Euston in 242 minutes on September 5, 1957, cutting 37 minutes off the schedule, and recording an average speed of 74mph. Although no record was taken apart from the guard's log, it has been said that the journey in some aspects bettered that in 1937 on which No. 6220 *Coronation* purportedly hit 114mph.

Outshopped from Crewe on July 12, 1937, No. 46244 was withdrawn on September 12, 1964.

No. 6231 acquired a following in the Forties because Hornby produced a very popular Dublo model of it. Having emerged from Crewe Works on June 28, 1938, it was withdrawn on December 29, 1962, and was among the first to be scrapped. ERIC TREACY/NRM

LMS PRINCESS CORONATION PACIFICS

NUMBER	NAME	ENTERED SERVICE	WITHDRAWN
6220*	Coronation	June 1937	April 1963
6221*	Queen Elizabeth	June 1937	May 1963
6222*	Queen Mary	June 1937	October 1963
6223*	Princess Alice	June 1937	October 1963
6224*	Princess Alexandra	July 1937	October 1963
6225*	Duchess of Gloucester	May 1938	September 1964
6226*	Duchess of Norfolk	May 1938	September 1964
6227*	Duchess of Devonshire	June 1938	December 1962
6228*	Duchess of Rutland	June 1938	September 1964
6229*	Duchess of Hamilton	September 1938	February 1964
6230	Duchess of Buccleuch	June 1938	November 1963
6231	Duchess of Atholl	June 1938	December 1962
6232	Duchess of Montrose	July 1938	December 1962
6233	Duchess of Sutherland	July 1938	February 1964
6234	Duchess of Abercom	August 1938	January 1963
6235*	City of Birmingham	June 1939	September 1964
6236*	City of Bradford	July 1939	March 1964
6237*	City of Bristol	August 1939	September 1964
6238*	City of Carlisle	September 1939	September 1964
6239*	City of Chester	August 1939	September 1964
6240*	City of Coventry	March 1940	September 1964
6241*	City of Edinburgh	April 1940	September 1964
6242*	City of Glasgow	May 1940	October 1963
6243*	City of Lancaster	May 1940	September 1964
6244*	King George VI	July 1940	September 1964
6245*	City of London	June 1943	September 1964
6246*	City of Manchester	August 1943	January 1963
6247*	City of Liverpool	September 1943	May 1963
6248*	City of Leeds	October 1943	September 1964
6249	City of Sheffield	April 1944	November 1963
6250	City of Lichfield	May 1944	September 1964
6251	City of Nottingham	June 1944	September 1964
6252	City of Leicester	June 1944	June 1963
6253	City of St Albans	September 1946	January 1963
6254	City of Stoke-on-Trent	September 1946	September 1964
6255	City of Hereford	October 1946	September 1964
6256	Sir William A Stanier FRS	December 1947	October 1964
46257	City of Salford	May 1948	September 1964

*Streamlined as built

and Perth on the main line routes, including service along the North Wales coast to Holyhead.

They made regular appearances at Shrewsbury, the short run from Crewe providing both a useful fill-in turn and also an ex-works running-in duty.

Most of the class were allocated almost exclusively to one of four 'Duchess' depots: 1B Camden, 5A Crewe North, 12B Carlisle Upperby and 27A Bank Hall (after 1948 66A).

Camden was the premier shed for the class. All new locomotives up to No. 6248 *City of Leeds* went there either immediately or within a short time of being outshopped. As more of the class were built, some of the earlier ones were switched to Crewe North and Polmadie.

Carlisle Upperby was the last depot to get a sizeable allocation, in 1946-47, following the allocation of the last five to Camden.

Indeed, Nos. 6248-52 were the only class members which did not begin their regular careers at Camden. Until the Second World War, all Princess Coronations were based there, and as late as the Fifties, other depots sent their Duchesses there during the summer.

There were also smaller allocations of the class to Edge Hill 8A and Holyhead 7C. Also, some Carlisle engines occasionally worked out of Kingmoor shed.

Camden shed closed in 1961, with the Duchesses still left in London being moved to Willesden shed.

Rebuilt No. 46227 in British Railways' Brunswick green at Preston in July 1961. Emerging from the works on June 7, 1938, along with Nos. 46231/2, it was one of the first three Duchesses to be withdrawn, on December 29, 1962. COLOUR-RAIL 300024

No. 6234 *Duchess of Abercorn* – the locomotive which set a record for a British steam locomotive by producing 3300hp during trials in 1939, and highlighted the true capability and awesome power of the Princess Coronation Pacifics – came out of Crewe Works on August 4, 1938. It is seen heading through Atherstone with the Down 'Caledonian' in September 1959. Its proven power meant that there were calls for it to be officially preserved as part of the National Collection when it was withdrawn on January 26, 1963, but very sadly they went unheeded. COLOUR-RAIL BRM651

Rebuilt former streamliner No. 46228 *Duchess of Rutland* thunders away from Lichfield (Trent Valley) on May 23, 1959. Appearing from Crewe on June 17, 1938, it was withdrawn on September 12, 1964. COLOUR-RAIL 300475

Outshopped on June 27, 1938, No. 6230 *Duchess of Buccleuch* was the first Princess Coronation Pacific to be built without streamlining. Pictured at Stewarton in Ayrshire as No. 46230, it was withdrawn on November 9, 1963. COLOUR-RAIL 305024

No. 6236 *City of Bradford* appeared on July 27, 1939, and in its rebuilt form, represented the class in the Locomotive Exchanges of 1948. It is seen at Farnborough on June 15 that year during the trials. It was withdrawn on March 14, 1964. T OWEN/COLOUR-RAIL 92810

When withdrawn on September 12, 1964, as one of the last survivors of the class, No. 46237 *City of Bristol* had run up an average mileage of 72,437, second only to No. 46239 *City of Chester*. It had appeared from Crewe on August 9, 1939. It is pictured heading through Newton Abbot on May 10, 1955. LF FOLKARD/COLOUR-RAIL 13914

No. 6241 *City of Edinburgh* came out of the works on April 3, 1940 as a streamliner. In the late Forties, it was repainted in British Railway express passenger blue livery. It is pictured at Camden shed in 1949. Its career ended with withdrawal on September 5, 1964, during which time it recorded an annual average mileage of 72,202, the third highest of any class member. W BOOT/COLOUR-RAIL BRM139

For trainspotters, the Duchesses were not the easiest of classes to complete. As with the Eastern Region A4s, many of their duties were nocturnal on the heavy sleeper services. Engine changing was prevalent at Crewe and more especially at Carlisle, thereby making the Scottish members of the class, for instance, a fairly rare sight at Euston.

COLOUR SCHEMES

The class has carried many livery variations. The streamlined versions appeared in both Caledonian blue – forever associated with the 'Coronation Scot' – and crimson lake, along with plain and LNWR black applied.

In 1946, No. 6234 *Duchess of Abercorn* was painted an experimental blue/grey by the LMS, while the same locomotive carried British Railways lined black in 1948.

Twenty-seven members of the class received British Railways express passenger blue before it was superseded by Brunswick green, which was first seen on No. 46232 *Duchess of Montrose* in November 1951.

Indeed, Brunswick green, adopted by the nationalised railway from the GWR, was the only livery to be carried by every member of the class. I wonder what Stanier, who had been lured away from the Swindon empire, would have made of that in his years of retirement?

British Railways experimental lined black livery was applied to Nos. 46226, 46234, 46238, 46246, 46248, 46251, 46252 and 46256.

In December 1957, red made a return as a locomotive colour when No. 46245 *City of*

No. 46239 *City of Chester* was the sole member of the class allocated to 7C Holyhead shed for any considerable period, as happened its final year before withdrawal. Built at Crewe as a streamliner and outshopped on August 29, 1939, it was withdrawn on September 12, 1964, having topped the class charts for average annual mileage with a figure of 76,256. It is pictured at Ashton with an Up parcels train on August 1, 1963. Scrapped after withdrawal, its original tender survives in preservation, having been exchanged with that of No. 6229 *Duchess of Hamilton* in 1945. K FAIREY/COLOUR-RAIL 306258

Despite its name, No. 46240 *City of Coventry*, outshopped as a streamliner on March 27 1940, was based in and around London throughout its working life. Indeed, it was one of the three class members in the capital, the others being No. 46243 and No. 46245. One of the last in service, it was withdrawn over the weekend of September 12, 1964. COLOUR-RAIL 307822

The last Princess Coronation Pacific to be destreamlined, No. 46243 *City of Lancaster* was painted straight into British Railways' express passenger blue once its drab wartime matt black casing was removed. It is seen heading for Llanfair PG station, otherwise known as Llanfairpwllgwyngyll or Llanfairpwllgwyngyllgogerychwyrndrobwllllantysiliogogogoch, Anglesey in August 1963. COLOUR-RAIL 300608

No. 46246 *City of Manchester* hauls the 'Midday Scot' Glasgow to Euston lunchtime express through Clifton Road Junction in April 1961. Having emerged from Crewe on August 11, 1943, as a streamliner, it underwent six boiler changes and was the last class member to lose its sloping smokebox, in 1960. It was withdrawn on September 12, 1964. COLOUR-RAIL BRM659/D SMITH

London re-emerged in the livery, to be followed by London Midland Region-based Duchesses Nos. 46225/6/8/9/36/8/40/3/4/7/8/51/4/6.

The shade of red (or maroon) varied and two styles of lining were applied. The final livery variant came with the application of the yellow cab stripe to some members of the class which signified that they could not work south of Crewe owing to limited overhead 25kV line clearance, as the electrification of the West Coast Main Line progressed northwards. Indeed, the yellow stripe on the cab may have been seen as the writing on the wall for the Duchesses, for within a short time of its being applied, the remainder of the class were withdrawn.

The Duchesses also had 'British Railways' lettering on the tender, the first and second BR tender totems, along with blue, red and black backed nameplates. The early BR crest was applied from 1949 and was replaced by the later crest from 1956.

The net result: the class had one of the most complicated livery histories of any.

NOT IMMEDIATELY DISPLACED BY DIESELS

In 1960, the steady arrival of English Electric Type 4s (Class 40 under the later TOPs designation) ousted Duchesses from front-line work despite the fact that the newcomers were less powerful than the engines that they displaced – a case of backward technology in the name of standardisation?

Shed allocations on January 1 that year were: Camden: Nos. 46221/39/40/2/5/7; Crewe North Nos. 46220/8/9/33/5/41/3/6/8/9/51/3/4; Carlisle Upperby: Nos. 46225/6/34/6-8/44/50/2/5-7 and Polmadie: Nos. 46222-4/7/30-2.

From the end of 1960, the decline of the Duchess was unstoppable.

A total of 200 Class 40s were built by English Electric at Vulcan Foundry in Newton-le-Willows between 1958-62, and in those early years they were the pride of the new British Railways' fleet.

However, direct comparisons on the Great Eastern main line showed that the diesels offered little advantage over British Railways' Britannia Pacifics. Accordingly, the

No. 46242 *City of Glasgow* is seen heading the Royal Train through Chester on July 4, 1957. New out of Crewe Works on May 15, 1940 as a streamliner, it became unique among the class after it was the only one of three engines involved in the 1952 Harrow & Wealdstone crash to survive. In 1957, it hauled the inaugural 'Caledonian' from Glasgow to Euston and back, the nearest that British Railways ever came to emulating the 'Coronation Scot' which lasted until 1964. During its working life, which ended on withdrawal on October 19, 1963, *City of Glasgow* had six boilers and nine tenders. COLOUR-RAIL 12261

Eastern Region refused to accept any more as they were considered unsuitable to replace steam on the East Coast Main Line, and opted to wait until the Class 55 production Deltics were available.

By contrast, the London Midland Region was only too pleased when the Eastern Region released the unwanted diesels. They were used to replace their ageing West Coast steam fleet, with the ability to run up Camden bank north of Euston with ease.

The West Coast Main Line had been starved of investment for many years and the poor track and general lower speeds, when compared with the East Coast Main line, better

suited Class 40 as the need to hold trains at speed for long periods simply did not exist. The route better exploited their fairly rapid acceleration.

But it was electrification that drove the final nail into the coffin of the Duchesses. The beginning of the end came in December 1962 when Nos. 46227/31/2 were withdrawn from Polmadie. Nos. 46234/46/53 followed in January 1963, the latter engine having been in service for only 17 years.

During the course of 1963, Nos. 46220-4/30/42/47/9/52 followed their classmates into retirement, and soon the scrapyard.

The beginning of 1964 saw Nos. 46229/33

DUCHESSES IN ACCIDENTS

JULY 21, 1945: No. 6231 *Duchess of Atholl* was hauling an express passenger train, which overran signals at Ecclefechan, Dumfriesshire, and collided with a freight train being shunted. Two people were killed and three injured.

APRIL 17, 1948: No. 6251 *City of Nottingham* was hauling a mail train which was in a rear-end collision with a passenger train at Winsford, Cheshire, killing 24 people. It was the first major accident for the newly nationalised British Railways.

APRIL 25, 1949: No. 46230 *Duchess of Buccleuch* was hauling a passenger train that overran a signal and was derailed at Douglas Park signalbox, Motherwell, Lanarkshire. The signalman was suspected of having deliberately moved points beneath the train.

OCTOBER 8, 1952: Hauling an express passenger train, No. 46242 *City of Glasgow* overran signals and crashed into a local passenger train at Harrow & Wealdstone, Middlesex. Another express passenger train ran into the wreckage. The second deadliest railway accident in Britain left 112 people dead, with a further 10 dying later from their injuries.

FEBRUARY 3, 1954: No. 46250 *City of Lichfield* was hauling a passenger train which derailed on a broken rail inside Watford Tunnel, Hertfordshire. The rear three carriages became divided from the train at Watford Junction station, one of them ending up on the platform. Fifteen people were injured.

Photographed at Camden shed, No. 46247 *City of Liverpool* was based in the capital throughout its working life. Outshopped on September 13, 1943, as a streamliner, it was withdrawn on May 25, 1963. G PARRY COLLECTION/COLOUR-RAIL 312236

Departing Edinburgh Princes Street On October 5, 1963 with a Railway Correspondence & Travel Society special is No. 46251 *City of Nottingham*. With West Coast Main Line electrification creeping north and dieselisation in full swing, this tour was seen as a last chance to travel behind a Princess Coronation Pacific. The train comprised 11 LMS coaches, and was due to have been hauled by No. 46256 *Sir William A. Stanier F.R.S.*, but had failed the previous week with a defect on the front bogie.
No. 46251 was therefore taken out of storage specially for this run and cleaned up. The trip was from Crewe to Edinburgh and back, with Fowler 2-6-4T, the Shap banker at that time, providing assistance up to the summit on the outward run. However, Beattock was conquered without assistance in both directions. The locomotive, which emerged from Crewe on June 30, 1944, was withdrawn on September 12, **1964.** AER COPE/COLOUR-RAIL SC194

No. 6248 was the second Princess Coronation 4-6-2 to be named *City of Leeds*, the first, No. 6244, having been changed to *King George VI*. No. 6244 emerged from Crewe on October 2, 1943, with a reconditioned as opposed to new boiler. In its rebuilt form, it was said to be the pride of Crewe North shed, and was always turned out in pristine fashion. It is seen in full flight passing Bailrigg near Lancaster. COLOUR-RAIL 3087856

sold off to holiday camp magnate Billy Butlin – as we will see in the chapters to follow.

After that, only No. 46236 was removed from service before British Railways decided that all remaining Duchesses should be withdrawn at the end of the 1964 summer service.

Duchess, Princess Coronation, 8P (a classification only acquired in British Railways' days) or semi, call them what you like, it is now half a century since the mass withdrawals, which at the time was thought would remove the class from our railway system for ever.

They were one of the iconic classes that along with the LNER A4s would always bring shouts of identification (and joy) from lineside spotters whenever they appeared.

Perhaps it was because both classes were instantly recognisable that they were singled out for adulation a little more than the Kings on the Western or the Merchant Navies on the Southern, or because the two classes had battled it out before the war for the title of fastest steam engine in the country.

There was, however, no avoiding the hard fact that the sudden withdrawal in September 1964 of a class of locomotive that was less than 30 years old was a major blow to LMS fans.

THE SEPTEMBER 1964 CULL
In their dying months, the enthusiasts recorded every move of each Duchess, but for the average spotter they were quite hard to seek out.

In August 1963, on some spotting trips, Nos. 46241/5 were seen at Euston on the 8th, Nos. 46233/45 at Rugby on the 12th, Nos. 46240 at Euston, Nos. 46225/33/45/56 on shed at Camden on the 14th, and Nos. 46238/40/45/54 on the 24th at Tamworth.

The Railway Observer reported that in April 1964, many Euston-Birmingham duties had reverted to steam haulage, with Nos. 46238/54 being noted in action. They continued on these turns through the summer with Nos. 46236/40/5/54/6/7 being noted in July.

But the majority of their work was on parcels and fitted freight along with last-minute diesel substitutions on front-line duties.

It was on summer Saturdays that the Duchesses returned to front-line duties. In both 1963 and 1964, north of Crewe, steam-hauled services still greatly outnumbered diesel duties. For instance, Nos. 46229/40/45/54 were noted on successive August Saturdays at the

head of the 'Lakes Express' at Preston.

Carlisle was a hotspot for the class: on July 16, 1963 between 7pm and 9.30pm, Nos. 46224/5/33/7/8/42 all appeared on passenger and parcels turns.

Despite being withdrawn in 1962, Nos. 46231/2 were still in store at Carstairs on this date. October and November 1963 were quiet months for the class, but members were back out in force for the parcels extras required in December. Several were then placed into storage at the start of January.

By the end of February 1964, Duchesses were clearly still needed. Five of the stored engines were back in traffic, and seven

Duchess No. 46250 *City of Lichfield* at Euston on April 22, 1960. Appearing from Crewe on April 19, 1944, it was one of the earliest class members to be withdrawn, on November 9, 1963, having got through six boilers in its career. COLOUR-RAIL BRM2806

No. 6249 *City of Sheffield* was the first of four streamliners ordered during the Second World War, which ended up being built minus the streamlining. It appeared from the works on April 19, 1944, and was withdrawn on November 9, 1963. Four months earlier, in a somewhat end-of-steam era grimy condition, it is seen departing Glasgow St Enoch with a flourish of steam. JB SNELL/COLOUR-RAIL 305047

The last of the 38 Princess Coronations, and the only one to be built by British Railways, was No. 46257 City of Salford, which like No. 6256 *Sir William A. Stanier F.R.S.*, was built to the Ivatt modified design. It had the shortest career of any Duchess, lasting just 16 years in service between its appearance from Crewe on May 19, 1948, and withdrawal on September 12, 1964. In 1956, it was loaned to the Western Region and like No. 46256, it briefly carried electric headlamps in latter times. In British Railways Brunswick green livery, it is seen on Wigan Springs Branch shed carrying a headboard welcoming 'Britain's Railway Queen.' A BURGESS/ COLOUR-RAIL 300769.

No. 6252 *City of Leicester* came out of Crewe Works on June 24, 1944, as the last of the four non-streamlined Princess Coronations to be built during World War Two. Seen conquering Shap in June 1962, it was among the first Duchesses to be withdrawn, its career ending on June 1, 1963. M SMITH/COLOUR-RAIL BRM2034

Duchess No. 6253 *City of St Albans* came out of the works on September 14, 1946. It was the first non-streamliner to have the new 'utility' front footplate together with a cylindrical smokebox, and also the first Duchess with a riveted tender. Seen powering through Kenton in April 1962, it was withdrawn the following January. M SMITH/COLOUR-RAIL BRM2035

members of the class were noted in Glasgow at the end of the month.

No. 46254 was seen at Aston (Birmingham) on February 28, at the head of the Condor fitted freight, while on Grand National day, Nos. 46228/39/40/51 all left Euston within half an hour heading race specials.

No. 46235 was seen on coal empties at Preston on April 7, with No. 46228 heading the 'Mid-day Scot' there the next day.

During the summer timetable, it appeared to be business as usual, with the 'Lakes Express', 'Merseyside Express' and 'Northern Irishman' all being hauled by Duchesses.

Was it just a coincidence that on September 4, 1964, a diesel 'failed' and No. 46238 worked the last Down Caledonian of the season?

THE FAREWELL TOUR

A week later and the class was no more except for No. 46256 *Sir William A. Stanier F.R.S.*,

rostered to work the Railway Correspondence & Travel Society's 'Scottish Lowlander' special on September 26.

Many of the locomotives had had a scandalously short working life. Indeed, the class as a whole averaged well less than 25 years in traffic.

The last trip by a Duchess in British Railways' service also involved two examples of the Princess Coronation Pacifics greatest rivals, Gresley's A4s. It was fitting that *Sir William A. Stanier F.R.S.* was therefore running with No. 60007 *Sir Nigel Gresley* on the trip.

The 'Scottish Lowlander' was organised to commemorate the passing of two of the steam era's greatest classes while visiting two secondary and threatened Scottish routes. The train comprised 12 coaches, totalling 450 tons gross.

The tour began at Crewe and started off behind headed by No. 46256 in its slightly fading maroon livery to Carlisle. There, the Duchess

and No. 60007 stood side by side for a few moments during the engine change, to the delight of all present.

No. 60007 took over, running on to the main line in the direction of Beattock.

No. 60007 then set back, in the Up direction on the Down Fast, to the signal controlling on the Waverley Route at Carlisle.

The A4 then headed the train over the Waverley Route through Hawick, Galashiels and on to Niddrie West Junction.

At Niddrie, it was found that the catering supplies for the buffet had run out. Staff ran off over the fields and bought everything they could find in terms of bacon, bread and butter from the nearest local shops.

From there, A4 No. 60009 *Union of South Africa* took the train via the Edinburgh Suburban Line to Glasgow St John's and via Kilmarnock and Dumfries back to Carlisle.

The performance of the all three Pacifics

Seen in ex-Crewe Works condition following overhaul, No. 46254 was one of two class members loaned to the Western Region – successor to the GWR where Stanier began his career – in 1956, the other being No. 46257 *City of Salford*. Outshopped from Crewe on September 17, 1946, it was withdrawn on September 12, 1964. G PARRY COLLECTION/COLOUR-RAIL 312233

The first of the two class members built to the 'improved' Ivatt design, No. 6256 *Sir William A. Stanier F.R.S.* appeared from Crewe on December 13, 1947, less than three weeks before nationalisation. With hindsight, there should have been every reason to preserve it following its withdrawal on October 3, 1964, if only for the illustrious name that it carried. It was the last Stanier Pacific to be withdrawn and was scrapped at Cashmore's yard in Great Bridge. It is seen exiting Primrose Hill tunnel. COLOUR-RAIL 12578

was superb. In particular, the run of No. 60007 over the Waverley Route – described as an all-time record for that line with that load – and that of No. 46256 on its last southbound run over Shap were praised.

What then, of the great Duchess sheds?

Camden, dating back to 1837 when it had been opened as a locomotive servicing facility at Chalk Farm for the London & Birmingham Railway, was closed to steam in December 1963. It was briefly used as a diesel depot until 1966, when it was demolished and replaced by sidings.

Polmadie shed had the second biggest allocation of the class, and which had been built by the Caledonian Railway in September 1875 to the west side of Rutherglen station on the north side of the Carstairs line, became a diesel depot after May 1967.

By the early Seventies, the rear through roads had been removed and the area converted to a car park. The coaling tower had also been demolished.

In 1975, the main shed was knocked down with only the two-road repair shop remaining in use as a maintenance workshop. The site is now occupied by Virgin Trains.

Crewe North, built by the LNWR in 1865, closed on May 24, 1965, and was demolished.

In 1948, the original LNWR shed at Carlisle Upperby Shed was swept away to be replaced by a roundhouse.

The shed, which had become 12B, closed to steam on December 12, 1966. The roundhouse was demolished in the Eighties. Upperby closed in the Nineties as a maintenance depot, but was still able to service preserved steam locomotives

Duchess No. 46255 *City of Hereford* heads the 'Caledonian' at Euston in March 1960. Appearing on October 16, 1946, it was the last of the pure Stanier design Princess Coronations. It was withdrawn on September 12, 1964. J MULLET/COLOUR-RAIL BRM404

running on the main line.

Today, it is a Traction Maintenance Depot used for storage of West Coast Main Line equipment. The depot code is now CL.

STANIER: THE LAST YEARS

And what of the designer of the Duchesses?

Despite retiring from the LMS, he continued his railway involvement, giving lectures, and serving as president of the Production Engineering Research Association from 1951-56, and was also on the board of the Royal Commission on Awards to Inventors.

In May 1956, the Institution of Mechanical Engineers held a lunch to mark his 80th birthday.

In 1958, Stanier became vice-president of the Stephenson Locomotive Society.

The Institution of Mechanical Engineers awarded him the James Watt International Medal, a year after he suffered a slight stroke.

He took regular holidays in Sidmouth, often visiting Oliver Bulleid, the designer of the great Southern Railway Pacifics, who lived nearby.

He died in Rickmansworth in September 1965, aged 89. His funeral was followed by a memorial service at St Margaret's, Westminster.

Including the 38 members of the Princess Coronation class, a total of 2726 Stanier locomotives were built between 1933-51. ■

LONDON MIDLAND ELECTRIFICATION

MANCHESTER – LIVERPOOL – CREWE – BIRMINGHAM – LONDON

STILL MAKING GOOD PROGRESS

The Duchesses were more powerful than the diesels originally brought in to replace them, but it was electrification that finally killed off the class.

CHAPTER SEVEN

DUCHESS OF HAMILTON:
A second life begins

No. 46229 *Duchess of Hamilton* departs
from York with BR's regular 'Scarborough
Spa Express' on August 12, 1984.
BRIAN SHARPE

Only one Princess Coronation Pacific was officially preserved for the nation, and that was No. 46235 *City of Birmingham*. Mainly because of its name, that city's local authority offered to display it inside its extended Museum of Science & Industry.

The other class members were destined for the scrapyard, regardless of their illustrious history.

Many of the heritage sector's iconic locomotives have been saved for future generations by unlikely players.

In 1963, Reading enthusiast Brian Walker was trying to drum up support among local authorities for classic LMS locomotives to be saved, but interest proved sparse, at first.

He hit upon the idea of writing to holiday camp magnate Billy Butlin at the company's London headquarters, asking for help with the funds that had been set up to save – successfully as it transpired – No. 46201 *Princess Elizabeth* and No. 46100 *Royal Scot*. He suggested that a place for saved locomotives might be found in the holiday camps.

Assistant managing director G S Ogg wrote back to say the company was prepared to provide space for rescued locomotives to be placed on public display.

But Butlins eventually went one better and decided that rather than support separate preservation campaigns, it would buy locomotives from British Railways itself.

Finding that *Princess Elizabeth* had been sold for preservation elsewhere, Butlins bought sister No. 46203 *Princess Margaret Rose*, for display at Pwllheli. The purchase was followed up by that of *Royal Scot*, which went to Skegness.

Butlins then asked the Eastern Region about LNER A4 pioneer No. 60014 *Silver Link* which was stored at Doncaster Works, but lost interest when a figure inflated way beyond the scrap price was asked for. The locomotive, which in 1935 achieved a speed of 112.5 mph – breaking the British record and sustaining an average of 100mph over a distance of 43 miles – accordingly, and disgracefully, went for scrap.

Much the same happened when Butlins asked about GWR 4-6-0 No. 6018 *King Henry VI*. Another would-be buyer was the actor Kenneth More, but the star of such films as Reach for the Sky and Genevieve pulled out when he heard that Butlins was interested.

Again, a price could not be agreed with Swindon, and Butlins looked elsewhere – More was said to have been distraught when he heard that the King had been scrapped.

Derby, however, proved far more receptive to Butlins than Swindon or Doncaster.

Mr Ogg inquired about the availability No. 46220 *Coronation* for its Minehead resort, because of its historic US trip. However, Brian Walker enlightened him to the fact that No. 6229 had been the locomotive that crossed the Atlantic, not the real No. 6220.

Butlins therefore chose No. 46229. *Duchess of Hamilton*, which was taken to Crewe Works for cosmetic restoration. On

Minus its smoke deflectors, No. **6229** *Duchess of Hamilton* is towed by GWR pannier No. **9647** along the Minehead branch en route to Butlins holiday camp in April 1964.

No. **6229** *Duchess of Hamilton* as a static exhibit at Butlins holiday camp in Minehead. It was displayed next to London, Brighton & South Coast Railway 'Terrier' 0-6-0T No. **32678** *Knowle,* which later returned to steam on the Kent & East Sussex Railway. ROBIN WEBSTER*

Duchess of Hamilton undergoing cosmetic restoration inside Swindon Works in 1976 after being retrieved from Butlins holiday camp at Minehead via the West Somerset Railway. JOHN TITLOW

April 24, 1964 it was moved south by rail to Minehead, completing the last stage of its journey being towed up the branch line to the resort behind GWR 0-6-0 pannier tank No. 9647, which did not survive into preservation.

Brian Walker then suggested that No. 46242 *City of Glasgow* could be bought for the Heads of Ayr holiday camp, but it was No. 46233 *Duchess of Sutherland* that was chosen, possibly because of the strong Scottish connections with the name.

Butlins displayed No. 6229 at Minehead from April 1964, and camp staff did their best to look after it, regularly greasing moving parts and applying aluminium paint to rods and motion, which helped delay corrosion.

However, you only have to look at the rows of rusting steam locomotives in Barry scrapyard to appreciate the effects of the salty air of the Bristol Channel over several years.

As the Crewe paint job began to fade, and interest among the young campers went following the passing of British Railways' main line steam, what had been a star attraction slowly turned into a burden as far as Butlins was concerned, and the holiday company was no longer keen to keep financing its maintenance.

No. 46229 *Duchess of Hamilton* departs from Scarborough with BR's regular 'Scarborough Spa Express' on August 19 1984. BRIAN SHARPE

NEW MUSEUM, NEW HOME

By 1970, Butlins had begun looking for new homes for the steam locomotives.

Eventually, the Science Museum and Butlins agreed a 20-year lease of No. 6229 which would see it restored cosmetically at Swindon Works and then transferred to the new National Railway Museum at York.

British Rail closed the Minehead branch in 1970, but the track was left in place because of moves to reopen it as the West Somerset Railway. After British Rail sent a diesel along it to ensure that it could still be used, it was decided to take No. 6229 out the way it had arrived – by rail.

On March 10, 1975, a low loader took it from the holiday camp to nearby Minehead station, the preparations for its journey helped by volunteers from the Dart Valley Railway.

Three days later, it was slowly hauled to Taunton behind Class 25 diesel No. 25059 and arrived at Swindon Works on March 17.

It was decided to restore *Duchess of Hamilton* in its final BR condition, so a new set of smoke deflectors was made as it had been displayed at Butlins without them.

The restoration took more than a year, and No. 46229 was unveiled at the new York museum on May 26, 1976, at a dinner held to mark the centenary of William Stanier's birth.

BACK IN STEAM

LMS expert and author the late David Jenkinson was a member of the museum's curatorial staff in the mid-Seventies, and it was he who proposed that money should be raised to return *Duchess of Hamilton* to steam.

In late 1976, he asked legendary railway painter Terence Cuneo to paint a portrait of No. 46229 climbing Beattock Bank and sold a limited edition of fine art reproductions.

The profits went into a special fund set up – and added to – by the Friends of the National Railway Museum.

The overhaul of the Duchess began in May 1978, but as the months and then years passed, many unforeseen problems were encountered and then solved... at expense.

Finally, May 1, 1980 saw it undertake a trial run.

Nine days later, the Duchess hauled two trains around the York-Leeds-Harrogate circle under the banner of the 'Limited Edition'. However, it had to be piloted by a diesel during a York to Carnforth run on May 17, because of the risk of fire during a drought.

No. 46229 was able to join the Rocket 150 cavalcade on May 24-26, celebrating the 150th anniversary of the Liverpool &

Manchester Railway, the world's first inter-city line.

On November 1, 1980, the Duchess made its eagerly awaited heritage-era debut on the Settle to Carlisle line, but stalled in bad weather of the climb past Stainforth, and needed assistance from the rear by Class 40 No. 40134.

On May 23, 1981, No. 46229 hauled the first 'Scarborough Spa Express' which was scheduled to run on summer Tuesdays and Wednesdays from York to the resort and back. This was following an agreement between the Eastern Region and Scarborough Borough Council, which saw a 60ft turntable from Gateshead installed at Scarborough, with financial assistance from the local authority. It was part of British Rail's Full Steam Ahead programme in 1981.

No. 46229 became a mainstay of steam motive power on the main line, at one stage being temporarily based at Marylebone, and running over routes that were new to the class. However, on October 26, 1985, it made a farewell trip with the 'Cumbrian Mountain Express' before its seven-year main line boiler ticket expired.

During its six years back on the network. No. 46229 covered a total of 13,223 miles.

No. 46229 *Duchess of Hamilton* crosses Knaresborough viaduct with a 'Scarborough Spa Express' on August 12, 1984. BRIAN SHARPE

No. 46229 Duchess of Hamilton at Steamtown Carnforth on April 10 1982. BRIAN SHARPE

Freshly overhauled at the National Railway Museum at York ready for its second seven-year stint on the main line, and with its paintwork not quite finished, No. 46229 *Duchess of Hamilton* tops Ais Gill summit on the Settle & Carlisle line on April 30, 1990. BRIAN SHARPE

A SECOND OVERHAUL

Extensive work on the boiler was needed if *Duchess of Hamilton* was to steam again. The museum gave the go-ahead for its friends group to restore it once more, and the boiler was duly lifted on May 6, 1986 and taken to the Oldham firm of C H Thomson Ltd for the necessary work to be completed under contract.

A new tender tank was made, increasing the water capacity by 1000 gallons through eliminating the space for two tons of coal.

Another problem arose with the completion of the electrification of the East Coast Main Line, staunch A4 territory of yesteryear.

In its original form a Duchess would not have been allowed under the wires, so new cab side sheets were fabricated and the safety valves had to be reduced in height. The end result was a locomotive which stood 13ft 1in above rail level, giving adequate clearance.

In 1987, the museum concluded a deal with Butlins to buy the locomotive outright, and at last it became part of the National Collection.

The boiler was lifted back into the frames on March 7, 1989, and No. 46229 resteamed on December 9 that year, at a special day for supporters at the York museum.

A boiler certificate was issued by the British Rail inspector after another steam test five days later.

The locomotive ran light engine from Derby for weighting and adjustment of springs on March 28, 1990, and successfully undertook a loaded test run to Sheffield the following day, after which a new main line certificate was awarded. The second overhaul had cost the friends group £225,000.

SECOND MAIN LINE COMEBACK

On Good Friday, April 13, 1990, *Duchess of Hamilton* returned to service hauling a Pullman train on a 280-mile return trip from York to Carlisle over the Settle and Carlisle line.

However, BR announced that No. 46229 had to be diesel-towed between York and Leeds.

As No. 47555 *The Commonwealth Spirit* towed No. 46229 and train under Holgate Bridge at the south end of York station, its comeback seemed pointless.

Yet moments later there was an explosive noise from No. 46229 and suddenly the Class 47 was unofficially being pushed! Unofficial, yes, but it was the beginning of something that seems to go with this engine.

Once free of the 47 at Leeds, No. 46229 made a workmanlike ascent of the Long Drag.

However, at that stage, caution was shown over the usage of the Duchess.

Main line runs were not very frequent and largely limited to the Settle and Carlisle line. Nonetheless, a trip with No. 46229 was always a sell-out and tour operators began to clamour for more trips.

Gradually opportunities increased, but during that first year, they were limited to the Settle & Carlisle line. Some 'Cumbrian Mountain Express' runs involved a one-way run with *Duchess of Hamilton* with other runs behind another locomotive, such as *Princess Elizabeth* or Jubilee 4-6-0 No. 45596 *Bahamas*.

In July 1991, *Duchess of Hamilton* returned to the North Wales Coast line. A season based at Crewe Heritage Centre resulted in trips to

Llandudno and Holyhead, to Shrewsbury and Hereford (by both the Wrexham and Whitchurch routes) and the infamous 'Red Rose', which was sometimes described as a crawl round the backside of Lancashire.

The purpose of the 'Red Rose' was to get locomotives from Crewe to Carnforth without using the obvious route, as steam was not allowed to go direct.

During that summer, high speeds were achieved on the North Wales Coast route, in particular the run from Llandudno Junction to Chester. If departure was behind schedule, then there was the danger of delaying the following service train.

With Crewe men driving their favourite locomotive, there was much smart running from Prestatyn to Chester Racecourse. Flint was a favourite place to see the look of total surprise on the faces of passengers awaiting the next coastal service as No. 46229 hurtled through with the whistle howling.

New ground for the class was covered towards the end of 1992 when the friends group chartered a train from York to Workington via Leeds and Carnforth, while early 1993 saw No. 46229 back on the Settle and Carlisle route.

By now the regular working of the 'Cumbrian Mountain Express' had switched its southern base for steam to Bradford Forster Square.

'FIFTEEN GUINEA SPECIAL' RE-RUN

To celebrate 25 years since the end of steam an attempt was made to re-run the landmark 1T57 'Fifteen Guinea Special' on August 11 that year. Gradually, by the time all the rearrangements had taken place, it became a super-version of the 'Cumbrian Mountain Express' from Leeds... with Duchess power!

Of course No. 46229 had been withdrawn five years before the end of steam, but Britannia Pacific No. 70013 *Oliver Cromwell*, which had run on that last day in 1968, was not available. In its place, No. 46229 performed faultlessly and the passengers were left very happy.

However, they were less happy on the 'Cumbrian Mountain Express' run of September 18.

The Duchess had just left Bradford when it was obvious that all was not well. Finally it came to a halt at Bell Busk in North Yorkshire. The silence that befell the whole train was such that you could hear a pin drop.

No. 46229 had not failed on a train since its return to steam in 1990 but this was serious. Eventually Class 47 D1962 (which was following to take the train back from Carlisle) buffered on at the rear and pushed the whole ensemble to Hellifield. There No. 46229 was placed in a siding and the train went north behind D1962.

The problem was a hot bearing and so No. 46229 had to return to York light engine at reduced speed overnight.

On August 28, 1994 the friends chartered the Duchess to run an echo of the much-lamented 'Scarborough Spa Express'. At the time, with British Rail having gone into serious death throes during Privatisation, it proved very difficult to arrange this train. Two straightforward runs from York to Scarborough

Duchess of Hamilton **receives attention from its support crew during a brief stop at snowbound Garsdale with the northbound 'Cumbrian Mountain Express' on February 21, 1993.** IAN R SMITH

should have been fairly simple. But it was anything but.

The stock, from Manchester, courtesy of Regional Railways, arrived late. From then on it seemed as if the train was there under sufferance.

The trip gave the friends such a bad experience that it was the last time the group chartered a full train. Nevertheless No. 46229 performed faultlessly and appetites were whetted for some longer runs. On December 17, a southbound 'Cumbrian Mountain

Express' helped get No. 46229 back in the swing.

Crewe and York were the main line operating bases for No. 46229 during 1995 after which a spell at the East Lancashire Railway in return for maintenance saw an interesting return to York. On March 30, 1996, No. 46229 hauled an ELR-sponsored train from Preston to Manchester Victoria, then via Standedge and Healey Mills to York and Scarborough. On the return the locomotive went back to its base at York.

Duchess of Hamilton **on a visit to the Great Central Railway in December 1995.** BRIAN SHARPE

No. 46229 *Duchess of Hamilton* **departs from Stratford-upon-Avon with a 'Shakespeare Express' dining train returning to Marylebone on September 22, 1985.** BRIAN SHARPE

OUT OF GAUGE

A Pathfinder Railtours' trip took the Duchess from York to Derby and Crewe on June 8, 1996, via Sheffield Midland (water stop) following a mishap with a goods train on the Old Line along which the tour was booked. The problem was that the trip did not have route clearance for Sheffield Midland. Fortunately nothing untoward happened.

The year also marked the start of some very interesting workings for No. 46229. The old fixed routes seemed to be abandoned by the tour operators in a bid to try out new itineraries.

It seemed as if anything was possible and that the new regime at Railtrack might allow all sorts to happen. However, that turned out not to be the case. On June 16, No. 46229 was booked to go to Holyhead, a route that had been travelled since 1990. However, Railtrack suddenly announced that No. 46229 was out of gauge west of Llandudno Junction.

The onus was on the museum's curatorial staff to produce original drawings to prove that it was in gauge. That day, the passengers sampled Class 47 power between Llandudno Junction and Holyhead.

Only three weeks later, however, matters were very different. On July 6, No. 46229 took a Pathfinder Railtours trip northwards out of Carlisle. It was the first time that a Princess Coronation had hauled a train in Scotland since 1964.

The Duchess followed the Glasgow & South Western route through Dumfries and Kilmarnock to Glasgow, but was not allowed access to Glasgow Central. Instead, the train travelled to Polmadie and was then was hauled back to Central by Class 47 No. 47572 *Ely Cathedral*.

Reversing its train under the signal gantry at Falsgrave, Scarborough, **No. 46229** *Duchess of Hamilton* **has just brought in a special from Preston while carrying a 'Scarborough Spa Express' headboard. The gantry has been relocated to Grosmont on the North Yorkshire Moors Railway where it now controls trains running from the heritage line into Whitby.** IAN R SMITH

No. 46229 *Duchess of Hamilton* passes Micklefield on the day of its return to service on May 10, 1980. BRIAN SHARPE

No. 46229 *Duchess of Hamilton* passes the grandstands at Rainhill during the Rocket 150 cavalcade marking the anniversary of the opening of the Liverpool & Manchester Railway. BRIAN SHARPE

Meanwhile No. 46229 had gone to Motherwell for servicing. Once the passengers had stretched their legs in Glasgow, the train was taken forward to Motherwell depot by Class 37 No. 37401 *Mary Queen of Scots*.

BEATTOCK AND SHAP

At last No. 46229 was to attempt the assault of Beattock Bank. This emotive climb was somewhat spoilt by the authorities deciding that the best place to water the locomotive between Motherwell and Carlisle was way up the bank at Abington.

The hose from the road tanker having an incompatible nozzle to that on the Duchess did nothing to improve matters, and the eagerly awaited climb up Beattock was a damp squib.

That summer was bedevilled with fire risk cancellations of main line steam. No. 46229 should have worked three trips on the Settle and Carlisle but these were denied. Instead a diesel tow was required to fulfil the booked appearance at the Crewe 150 celebrations on August 17.

October 19, 1996 will be remembered as the day No. 46229 returned to Shap. Heading a Days Out railtour from Crewe to Carlisle and back, it was the first time it had hauled a train over the northern part of the LNWR main line since 1963.

It was explosive. Racing through Carnforth, where unique BR 8P Pacific No. 71000 *Duke of Gloucester* was on hand to give a supportive whistle, the Duchess was soon hard at work

No. 46229 *Duchess of Hamilton* departs from Skipton on November 1, 1980 on its first run in preservation over the Settle & Carlisle line. It was to stall at Stainforth and required assistance from Class 40 diesel No. 40134. BRIAN SHARPE

climbing the Lakeland fells. Roaring up to Dillicar, a temporary restriction resulted in a slackening of speed to Tebay. Then it was on to the final slog.

From passing Tebay, speed increased for some time before the gradient began to bite back.

The crowds who waited to see the train go past were not disappointed as No. 46229 shouted defiantly at the fells, before surmounting the summit at 57mph.

SPEED RECORD

Following a brief visit to the Mid Hants Railway, which saw No. 46229 also reach Bristol, Reading and Exeter, the end of November saw the final main line run.

Labelled the 'Royal Scot', this Days Out trip took in the entire West Coast Main Line from Euston to Glasgow on November 30, and then the East Coast route from Glasgow to York on December 1.

A Class 47 was attached behind the tender both as 'insurance' and for train heating.

In the event it came in useful.

The northbound run was spectacular. It was driver Les Jackson's last day at work before retirement, and he was determined that he and the Duchess would go out in style.

It was on this journey that No. 46229 gained its reputation as the fastest British steam locomotive in preservation at that time.

The calibrated speedometer on the Class 47 verified that between Shap and Carlisle, a very high speed indeed was recorded.

It was never officially made public, but was in excess of the then permitted maximum of 60mph. The 560-ton load was hauled over the 85.5 miles from Barton Loop to Carlisle in 83 minutes 10 seconds at an average of 61.7mph.

The next day, the last for No. 46229 on its main line ticket, saw a chapter of delays occur. The worst was a three-hour delay in the

In the newly rebuilt confines of Manchester Victoria, No. 46229 works a Preston-Scarborough train on March 30, 1996 as a means of returning the engine to York following a spell on the East Lancashire Railway. IAN R SMITH

No. 46229 *Duchess of Hamilton* performs a photographic runpast over Ribblehead Viaduct for passengers on a southbound 'Cumbrian Mountain Express' on June 9, 1984. BRIAN SHARPE

Newcastle area which resulted in the locomotive running short of water for the last dozen miles into York. That 47 had its uses, such as when it opened its throttle, allowing No. 46229 to coast into York. However, it was a sad ending for a distinguished main line stint.

The following months saw No. 46229 visit the Mid Hants, the Nene Valley and the East Lancashire.

At the latter, it was agreed that No. 46229 could be painted in BR Brunswick green for enthusiast photographic charters as long as it was repainted in crimson before being returned to York.

Its final day in service, March 21, 1998, saw it hauling trains between Bury and Rawtenstall every even numbered hour from 10am until 6pm. One run was double-headed with LNER A4 Pacific No. 60007 *Sir Nigel Gresley*, an inconceivable combination in the days of steam but one with immense novelty value for those who travelled.

Withdrawn at the peak of performance, it was intended to overhaul No. 46229 back to operational condition, but various issues at the end of the Nineties meant that proposed financing of the work never materialised.

Yet in the 21st century, another big adventure awaited the Duchess... this time as a static exhibit. ∎

West and East Coast steam supreme! On its last day in steam, March 21, 1998, No. 46229 *Duchess of Hamilton* lines up alongside A4 Pacific No. 60007 *Sir Nigel Gresley* at Rawtenstall on the East Lancashire Railway. IAN R SMITH

A storming performance from green-liveried *Duchess of Hamilton* during an otherwise dull and overcast February 25, 1998. FRED KERR

Briefly carrying BR green livery, No. 46229 *Duchess of Hamilton* passes Burrs on the East Lancashire Railway in February 1998. IAN R SMITH

Sunset at the end of a superb first day back on the main line: *Duchess of Sutherland* at the Midland Railway-Butterley's Swanwick Junction platform, after setting down passengers from its light engine proving run over the Sheffield circuit on July 4, 2001. ROBIN JONES

SUTHERLAND'S LONG ROAD BACK

Duchess of Hamilton built up a huge following during its heritage era career on the main line.

Especially among those who considered it to be an example of the finest locomotive type built in Britain, its withdrawal and uncertain future left the sector so much poorer.

However, by the time that No. 46229 was making its last trips in Brunswick green livery on the East Lancashire Railway, moves were well advanced to fill the void that it would leave, in the form of the second Duchess that Billy Butlin had saved from the scrapyard.

Built at Crewe in July 1938, No. 6233 *Duchess of Sutherland* was the only one of the three preserved class members that was never streamlined.

Painted in LMS standard crimson lake livery, it had a single chimney and no smoke deflectors.

It was first allocated to Camden shed. A double chimney was fitted in March 1941 and smoke deflectors were added in September 1945 because of drifting smoke.

It was painted in postwar LMS black livery in September 1946.

At nationalisation on January 1, 1948, it was allocated to Crewe North depot, and renumbered 46233 in October 1948. It was repainted in BR Brunswick green livery five years later.

In June 1958, it was allocated to Carlisle Upperby before eventually being withdrawn from Edge Hill depot in February 1964.

During its 25 years in service, No. 46233 ran around 1,650,000 miles – the second highest mileage by any member of the class.

Like *Duchess of Hamilton*, No. 46233 escaped the cutter's torch thanks to Billy Butlin, who bought it from British Railways. Minus its smoke deflectors, it was cosmetically restored at Crewe Works.

It was moved to Greenan Siding on the Heads of Ayr branch on September 15, 1964, behind LMS 'Black Five' 4-6-0 No. 45026, arriving early the following day.

In late October, an elaborate road-rail move saw the locomotive, along with London,

Brighton & South Coast Railway 'Terrier' 0-6-0T No. 32662 *Martello*, arrive at the holiday camp.

At Minehead, Butlins hired former drivers to explain the control and operation to thousands of youngsters who climbed up the set of access steps to board the cab each summer. The camp also became a magnet for enthusiasts who wished to glimpse a rare surviving example of a magnificent class.

However, as with *Duchess of Hamilton*, maintenance became a costly business, and interest dwindled as youngsters related less to the steam eras. As far as Billy Butlin was concerned, it was time for the locomotives to move on again.

A NEW HOME IN NORFOLK

Steam had found a precious bolthole in Norfolk. At a time when preservation sites were still few and far between, horticulturist Alan Bloom set up his own transport museum at Bressingham Hall at Diss in Norfolk. He moved to Bressingham in 1946, after selling his previous 36 acre site at Oakington in Cambridgeshire to

No. 6233 Duchess of Sutherland and LBSCR A1X 'Terrier' 0-6-0T No. 32662 Martello on display at Butlins' Heads of Ayr holiday camp in the sixties. COLOUR-RAIL.COM

raise the capital for the 220 acres, which he developed into a major nursery business.

He was a plant expert of international renown, particularly in the field of hardy perennials. He was also a transport enthusiast, with an interest in both rail and road steam engines.

On part of the site, he eventually laid four railway lines – a 9¼in miniature railway, a 2ft gauge circuit, a 15in gauge miniature railway… and a short length of standard gauge running line.

Largely as a result of the initiative of Bressingham staff member Geoffrey Sands, who had worked for British Railways and whose father had been chief traction inspector in the eastern region's Norwich District, efforts were made to secure LMS 4-6-0 No. 6100 *Royal Scot*, which had become an eyesore at Butlins' Skegness camp.

Alan approached Butlins, and in 1970, the company's board decided to release all of its locomotives to new good homes. While *Duchess of Hamilton* (Minehead) and Princess Royal 4-6-2 No. 46203 *Princess Margaret Rose* (Pwllheli) had already been advertised in attractions in the 1971 brochure, and could therefore not be moved until the end of season, those at Skegness and Heads of Ayr could be.

In February 1971, it was agreed No. 6100 and No. 6233 should go to Bressingham.

On March 16, 1971, Alan announced that both had been placed on permanent loan to his museum, a charitable trust.

On February 24, 1971, No. 6233 was taken from the holiday camp to Townhead sidings, the nearest railing site. It left there by rail just after noon on March 1, hauled by Class 27 diesel D5355. *Sutherland* eventually reached Bressingham on March 21. It was also joined by two other Butlin's engines, 'Terrier' *Martello* and LSWR B4 0-4-0T dock tank No. 102 *Granville*, as well as *Royal Scot*, bringing Alan's collection up to 38 steam vehicles.

Between 1972-74, *Duchess of Sutherland* was restored to working order at Bressingham,

the boiler needing major repairs. It first ran on the 500-yard demonstration line on May 28, 1974, when it was officially relaunched into traffic by none other than the Countess of Sutherland, who was also chairman of the Trentham Horticultural Centre.

Two days later, No. 6233 began giving footplate rides to the public.

It was withdrawn in 1976, mainly because of the deteriorating condition of the firebox tubeplate. It was estimated that repairs costing around £12,000 were needed, so it was decided to leave it as a static exhibit, a decision confirmed the follow year when Butlins said it would not contribute to the work.

For the next quarter of a century, the maroon-liveried locomotive continued to be a major attraction at Bressingham.

Meanwhile, after taking over Butlins, Rank Leisure Industries decided to sell off all of the locomotives. Accordingly, Nos. 6100 and 6233 were offered to Alan, and No. 6229 to the National Railway Museum. After protracted negotiations, *Duchess of Sutherland* was offered to Alan for £100,000, with the other three Butlins locomotives on the site free of charge. They were safe at last.

To mark the 25th anniversary of the end of steam in the north west in August 1993, No. 6233 went to the East Lancashire Railway on loan, and its identity was temporarily changed to No. 2000 *City of Manchester* as part of the city's abortive bid to stage the 2000 Olympic Games.

East Lancashire officials talked about taking No. 6233 on long-term loan and restoring it to working order, and offered to buy it for £100,000. Bressingham trustees declined.

Not exactly the West Coast Main Line – yet *Duchess of Sutherland* is still entertaining crowds as it moves up and down the Bressingham Steam Museum demonstration track.
MICHAEL ALDERMAN

A technical survey of the locomotive was commissioned with a view to taking it on a 10 year lease instead, but eventually the railway decided that it could not afford the restoration cost and hire fee. No. 6233 was taken back to Bressingham by road lorry on July 18, 1994, and went back on static display.

A NEW OWNER

In late 1994, Bressingham asked the Princess Royal Class Locomotive Trust, which is based in the West Shed at Swanwick Junction and what was then known at the Midland Railway Centre, if anyone was interested in buying the 9¼in garden line which included a Princess Royal-style Pacific named *Princess* and which was to be replaced with a new 10¼in version.

PRCLT chairman Brell Ewart discussed the full-size No. 6233.

When the Bressingham trustees decided to sell No. 6233 the following year, after the Health and Safety Executive had banned footplate rides leading to a future restoration being an economic non-starter, Brell was the first person to be contacted.

The trustees have been impressed with the PRCLT, its West Shed facilities and the restoration on its former Butlins engine Princess Royal No. 46203 *Princess Margaret*.

A sale price was provisionally agreed.

At the same time, the Great Central Railway had enquired about hiring No. 6233 for static display. The request was turned down, but the line came back with an offer to buy it, over and above what had been agreed with Brell.

Nonetheless, Bressingham trustees agreed in November 1995 to sell No. 6233 to Brell. A statement from Bressingham said: "The sale is in the best interests of the locomotive and the museum."

Brell's construction firm Whitehouse Construction, based at Ashbourne in Derbyshire, bought the locomotive while the PRCLT began raising money to pay for it.

Duchess of Sutherland left Bressingham for the last time on February 3, 1996. Alan Bloom

LMS 4-6-2 No. 6233 *Duchess of Sutherland* **giving a footplate ride on the Bressingham Steam Museum demonstration line in the mid-Seventies.** MICHAEL ALDERMAN

was so sad at the loss of the centre's flagship that he stayed indoors because he did not want to see it leave.

THE LOTTERY WIN

From the outset, the Princess Royal Class locomotive Trust intended to return *Duchess of Sutherland* to the main line.

The overhaul began soon after No. 6233 arrived at the West Shed, with the removal of the asbestos lagging blankets from the boiler and firebox, after being given special dispensation from the relevant authorities.

During 1997, after Whitehouse Construction indicated that it did not wish to continue with

the temporary ownership of No. 6233, an application was made to the Heritage Lottery Fund, at Brell Ewart's suggestion, covering both the purchase and the overhaul.

Meanwhile, two American businessmen expressed interest in buying No. 6233 to take it across the Atlantic, maybe forever. In June 1998, the trust was told that the Lottery bid had been successful. A grant of £324,508 covering 75% of the £432,677 project had been awarded.

History was to show that the restoration of No. 6233 would be one of many cases in which the Heritage Lottery Fund has been a major benefactor to the heritage railway movement.

The Lottery insisted that the project should

No. 6233 *Duchess of Sutherland* **heads over the stupendous 82-arch Harringworth Viaduct in Northamptonshire on its first and last trip to St Pancras with 'The Midlander' on December 8, 2000.** MIKE SPENCER

Approaching the later stages of its overhaul in the Princess Royal Class Locomotive Trust's West shed workshops is No. 6233 *Duchess of Sutherland.* ROBIN JONES

start in August that year, so on July 21 an official unveiling ceremony for the restoration took place in the West Shed, with the project team being announced. It comprised Brell as project leader, Eric Riley as chief engineer, Brian Radford as consulting engineer, Barrie Wheatley and Mick Boothby as steam fitters and John Riley and Graham Oulsnam as skilled fitters.

Firstly a new set of smoke deflectors – the originals had been fitted in 1946 – were made and trial fitted.

In autumn 1998, the boiler was lifted off and placed on accommodation bogies using a 75 tonne rail crane. The boiler was then taken to the Severn Valley Railway's Bridgnorth workshops for overhaul. The wheelsets also went there for turning, the three driving sets having returned by November 1998.

The tender tank was sent to the Ashbourne firm of Hill & Webster for refurbishment and an extension to the water space.

Air braking was installed, and new cladding sheets were made for the boiler barrel and firebox, using the old ones as patterns. Complete with the new cladding sheets and ashpan, the boiler was lowered on to the frames on July 28, 2000.

Automatic Warning System apparatus was installed, a first for an LMS air-braked locomotive cab layout. Also to comply with Railtrack Group Standards, the cab front and side windows were fitted with new laminated safety glass, replacing the original quarter-inch plate.

STEAMING AGAIN

The first fire at the West Shed was lit inside No. 6233 after it was hauled outside on January 17, 2001. It moved under its own power for the first time in PRCLT ownership the next day. It was the first time since 1976 that it had moved. It made a series of slow speed return trips on the Midland Railway Centre's main running line, still minus its smoke deflectors.

The final task was to complete the locomotive's repainting into the original Midland Red special livery used for the five original non-streamlined Princess Coronation locomotives when they were outshopped from Crewe in 1938. It therefore appeared again in its LMS era identity as No. 6233, rather than its latter-day No. 46233.

At the time, the locomotive carried a temporary nameplate displaying the PRCLT's website.

The boiler cladding receives the final touches at the West Shed. ROBIN JONES

LMS magnificence: *Duchess of Sutherland* **proudly stands at Sheffield during its July 4, 2001, proving run.** JAMES SHUTTLEWORTH

At a meeting with Railtrack, the predecessor to Network Rail, the date of July 4, 2001, was fixed for a light test run on the national network, and July 18 for the loaded test run.

At 11am on July 4, No. 6233 coupled to support coach No. 99041 and special saloon No. 6320, was given the green light at Codnor Park Junction where the Midland Railway Centre's line then connected with the national network.

A two-hour delay was caused by a points failure at Pye Bridge Junction, No. 6223 eventually completing two runs round the Derby-Chesterfield-Beighton-Sheffield-Erewash Valley circuit, 200 miles being needed to complete the required number of brake applications.

It was a success, and the culmination of a 900 day restoration project involving more than 25,000 man hours, including 15,000 by volunteers.

Sadly, the July 18 loaded test run, held 63 years to the day that No. 6223 had left Crewe Works, did not go so well. A faulty air pump led to No. 6233's failure on the trip, the 'Night Owl', with 700 passengers on board the 14-coach train.

The train ground to a halt 100 yards south of Dronfield station on the Derby-Sheffield 'test circuit', after the Duchess excelled in its climb up Sheffield's Heeley Bank.

The engine crew called Derby for a tow back to the tour's Midland Railway Centre starting point, and Fragonset sent Class 45 Peak diesel No. 45112 *The Royal Army Ordnance Corps*, which was waiting to make its main line return on a Preston-Penzance run two days later.

The total delay was around 90 minutes and the sell-out tour returned to Derby at 1.40am.

The pump and other components were subsequently dismantled to find the exact cause of the failure, which happened as the steam supply was cut off from the air brake. The fault

No. 6233 *Duchess of Sutherland* **heads along the Dawlish sea wall with Past Time Rail's 'The Mayflower' from Bristol to Plymouth on October 27, 2001. It followed the journey taken by sister Duchess** *City of Bradford* **in the 1948 locomotive exchanges.** JOHN F STILES.

was next day discovered to be too tight a fit of the piston in the shuttle valve on the air compressor, and it was modified to give more clearance.

Brell Ewart stressed that the outing had been a 'test' run – and the locomotive had otherwise turned in a five-star performance. The lineside had been thronged by sightseers for the evening trip, but failing light and worsening weather hampered photography.

However, the Duchess was fully certified and became No. 98834 on the TOPS system, the 98 indicating that it was a private locomotive, the 8 a Class 8 and the 34 the nearest available two numbers to the last two of the locomotive.

On September 6, 2001, Stanier's grandson Mike Stanier officially rededicated *Duchess of Sutherland* in a ceremony at Butterley station.

No. 6233 *Duchess of Sutherland* **on the afternoon of March 21, 2001.** ROBIN JONES

September 16 saw No. 6233 as star guest at Bombardier's Central Rivers depot, Barton-under-Needwood, open day.

Four days later, No. 6233 returned to the Severn Valley Railway, where its boiler and wheelsets had been overhauled. Along with former East Coast rival A4 No. 60009 *Union of South Africa*, it topped the bill at the September 21-23 steam gala, helping to make it the line's most successful event since 1986.

The figure of 7561 paying passengers for the event fell short of the 8000 recorded for the first visit of A3 Pacific No. 4472 *Flying Scotsman* 15 years before. The attendance figure helped reverse the effect of that year's nationwide outbreak of foot and mouth disease on passenger numbers up to June that year.

The rake behind the Duchess included seven LMS maroon coaches.

BACK ON THE MAIN LINE

The first proper main line runs for No. 6233 were on Sunday, October 14, 2001, with 'The North Wales Coronation' and October 21 with 'The Ynys Mon Duchess', hauling Rivera Trains' Mk.1 coaching set from Crewe to Holyhead and back. As will be described in the next chapter, there was a hidden purpose for these trips.

When No. 60009 *Union of South Africa* became unavailable at short notice for Past Time Rail's 'The Mayflower' from Bristol to Plymouth on October 27, No. 6233 deputised.

The 10 coach train was to be the heaviest to run over the route in the heritage era behind one steam locomotive. A Duchess had run over the South Devon banks during the Locomotive Exchanges of 1948 and so a return visit was eagerly anticipated. *Duchess of Sutherland* did not disappoint, turning in a blemishless performance.

No. 6233 proved a big hit on the Past Time Rail's 'Midlander' trip from Derby to St Pancras

Still minus nameplates, No. 6233 *Duchess of Sutherland* **is seen in steam at the Midland Railway-Butterley in a snowbound March 2001, at the start of two days of running tests.** ROBIN JONES

Steam salute: the cooling towers of Ratcliffe-on-Soar Power Station acknowledge the magnificence of No. 6233 *Duchess of Sutherland* as it heads 'The Midlander' to St Pancras on December 8, 2001. JAMES SHUTTLEWORTH

Brell Ewart, chairman of the Princess Royal Class Locomotive Trust, Gill Gardner, chairman of the Heritage Lottery fund's East Midlands committee and Mike Stanier, grandson of Sir William Stanier, at the official rededication of No. 6233 *Duchess of Sutherland* at Butterley station on September 6, 2001. COLIN TYSON

Duchess of Sutherland at Liverpool Lime Street with Pathfinder Tours' 'The Yorkshire Coronation' on March 9, 2002. FRED KERR 6233-200204

via Harringworth Viaduct and Kettering on December 8, 2001. The first time a Duchess had visited Kettering, many locals turned out to the station to see No. 6233 take on water.

No. 6233 stretched it legs and arrived on the outskirts of the capital some 25 minutes early, only to suffer a 16 minute delay outside St Pancras awaiting a platform.

It was the only time that a Duchess had visited St Pancras, and probably the last time too, as the station was subsequently transformed into St Pancras International, the Eurostar terminal.

A week later, No. 6233 became only the second member of its class in the heritage era

to visit Euston, the first, of course, being *Duchess of Hamilton*.

On Saturday, December 15, it hauled the outward portion of 'The Capital Duchess' railtour, steaming up Camden Bank before taking the Great Western main line through Oxford, Banbury, Dorridge and Tamworth before arriving at Derby.

March 9, 2000, saw No. 6233 haul 'The Yorkshire Coronation' from Liverpool Lime Street to York, recalling the days when Coronation Pacifics including No. 46233 were allocated to Edge Hill shed, and 11 days later took 'The Coronation Owl' a trip run by the PRCLT's operating arm Princess Margaret Rose Tours,

from Derby to Crewe via Stafford and Lichfield.

Saturday, April 13, 2002, saw No. 6233 head 'The Blackpool Duchess' from Derby to Blackpool via Stoke-on-Trent.

However, the trip that all linesiders had desperately wanted to see was *Duchess of Sutherland* take on Shap summit.

PMR Tours arranged 'The Citadel Express' for Saturday, April 20, diesel hauled from Birmingham International to Crewe, from where No. 6233 took the train on to Carlisle and back to Crewe via the legendary summit.

Exactly a week later, a second trip began diesel-hauled to Northampton, picking up at Rugby and Stafford en route to Crewe, where

No. 6233 *Duchess of Sutherland* passes Leyland en route from Blackpool North to Sheffield on April 13, 2002. FRED KERR

the Duchess again takes charge for the jaunt to Carlisle and back.

The last time that No. 6233 ran over Shap was on October 5, 1964, when it was ignominiously towed by a 'Black Five' to Scotland en route to Butlins' Heads of Ayr holiday camp, where it had for so long seemed destined to spend the rest of its days as a static exhibit gracefully rusting away.

Prior to that, its last fully-fledged run in traffic over Shap was in 1963.

After taking on water at Carnforth, the northbound leg gave No. 6233 the opportunity to show just what it could do.

Following an impressive climb of Grayrigg, it ascended Shap summit with the best-ever recorded time by a preserved steam locomotive, 5 mins 32 secs for the stretch between mileposts 31½ and 37¼ at an average speed of 62.4mph.

Sadly, the second Shap trip was less impressive.

No. 6233 developed noticeable steaming problems early into its journey, and was placed inside the loop at Greyrigg for a blow-up before tackling the climb from Tebay and the ensuing 4½ miles at 1-in-75, up through Scout Green to Shap summit.

The 'poke and blow' approach succeeded in bringing the fire round, the engine holding its own with 40mph indicated on the speedometer as the train went over the top.

It was not quite as dashing, as the previous week when the 4-6-2 took the same train over the summit, but it was good enough to see the train into Carlisle. There, it arrived just as LMS Stanier 8F 2-8-0 No. 48151 left with the steam-hauled leg of a Green Express Railtours trip from Llandudno to Sellafield.

On arrival at Carlisle, it was evident that the Duchess was still below par when serviced at London Road depot. Driver Bill Andrews said that he believed there was a problem with the engine, and it was then that closer inspection

Duchess of Sutherland at St Pancras on December 8, 2001. MIKE SPENCER

revealed a leaking seam just above the firebox hole.

Rather than place the locomotive at risk on the return trip, train operator the West Coast Railway Company suggested that the two Class 31 diesels under its auspices, Nos. 31452 and 31602, coincidentally running light to Carnforth to take the Green Express trip back to Llandudno, should work to accompany the 4-6-2.

Having shunted the stock to reform the train for the return journey, No. 6233 was joined by the 31s for the 28 mile climb back up through Calthwaite, Clifton, Shap to the summit before taking advantage of favourable gradients over the remaining 31 miles to Carnforth.

The two diesels came off at Carnforth to fulfil a Sellafield return working duty whereupon West Coast produced a third Class 31, No. 31128, to pilot the 4-6-2 and train on to Crewe, from where 'The Citadel Express' departed for Northampton.

Despite the problems, the train ran exactly to time. The leaking seam inside the firebox of *Sutherland* was recaulked the following day and on April 29, the engine and support coach were worked back to base via Stoke-on-Trent.

No. 6233 was soon back in action, taking PMR Tours' 'The Scarborough Coronation' from Leicester to Scarborough travelling via Chesterfield, Pontefract and York on May 11.

By then, news of a far more illustrious trip had been broadcast, one that would immortalise *Duchess of Sutherland* and its owning group in preservation history. ■

CHAPTER NINE

SUTHERLAND'S
ROYAL TRAIN FIRST

LMS Princess Coronation Pacific No. 6233 *Duchess of Sutherland* leaves Holyhead at 12.51pm on June 11, 2002, with the empty Royal Train en route to Llandudno Junction.

When the Princess Royal Class Locomotive Trust's immaculately restored No. 6233 *Duchess of Sutherland* hauled the Royal Train with both the Queen and the Duke of Edinburgh on board, trust chairman Brell Ewart described it as: "The proudest moment of my life in preservation."

The momentous journey, which saw the train travelling along the North Wales coast line from Holyhead to Crewe, took place on Tuesday, June 11, 2002.

The landmark event had taken a year of intensive planning under a veil of utmost secrecy.

There was no doubt in the minds of the three-man team wholly responsible for planning the 1938-built Class 8P locomotive's part in the national Golden Jubilee tour – Matthew Golton, general manager of EWS' Rail Express Systems, special services manager David Brown and Brell himself – that every second of it was well spent.

For the footplate crew, the big event began at 5.50am the day before, when No. 6233 steamed out of its West Shed home at Swanwick Junction arriving at Crewe Heritage Centre around 9am. There it was coaled and watered behind a steel fence of security. It then left Crewe for the Valley nuclear flask loading point four miles east of Holyhead around noon, arriving at 3pm with its support coach, BR Mk.1 BCK No. 99041, now repainted in matching LMS maroon.

However, it was not until 5.20am the following day that it backed on to the eight-coach Royal Train comprising carriages Nos. 2921, 2903, 2904, 2918, 2923, 2917, 2915 and 2920, with EWS Class 47 No. 47787 *Windsor Castle* on the rear.

Her Majesty had spent the night on board the train in readiness for her tour the following day. The Queen's and Duke of Edinburgh's saloons were built in 1972 and converted for royal use for the 1977 Silver Jubilee.

It was the first time in 35 years that steam had been used on the Royal Train.

For security reasons, the timings did not become apparent until the day itself, although hundreds of people gathered on the lineside in the hope of getting pictures.

The train was due at Llanfair PG (otherwise known as Llanfairpwllgwyngyllgogerychwyrndrobwllllan tysiliogogogoch, the station with the longest name in Britain) at 10am, but arrived two minutes early.

The royal couple stepped out of the train to resounding cheers from the flag-waving crowd before Matthew Speight, a pupil from Ysgol Gynradd Llanfairpwll, presented the Queen with a posy of flowers, as the Menai Bridge Band provided background music.

The royal party then left by car for Beaumaris Castle, visiting a local craft fair as a 21-gun salute was fired at the Royal Anglesey Yacht club by the Army to greet it.

Afterwards, the party left for Bangor where the Queen and Duke of Edinburgh attended a multi-faith service at Bangor Cathedral where Welsh Assembly First Minister Rhodri Morgan was also present.

Headed by No. 6233 *Duchess of Sutherland*, the Royal Train passes Old Colwyn on the Llandudno Junction to Crewe leg of the journey on June 11, 2002.

Following the service, the Queen headed for lunch at Penrhyn Castle, a National Trust property famed for its collection of locomotives and stock from narrow gauge slate lines in North Wales. Afterwards, she watched the Clwyd Inter-County Sports Event and Festival of Youth at Colwyn Bay.

Meanwhile, the Royal Train had carried on to Bangor, where it stood in the centre road for half an hour before the diesel hauled it back to Holyhead for servicing.

REBOARDING AT LLANDUDNO JUNCTION

It then set out again behind No. 6233, this time for Llandudno Junction, where it arrived at 2.04pm, and staff waited for nearly two-and-a-half hours for the royal party to arrive and embark again.

On the platform, Brell presented the Queen with a replica headlamp made by John Beesley at his Berkhamsted workshop with a brass plaque carrying the Jubilee motif. In return,

Brell received an engraved plaque commemorating the event.

"She said that she thought the locomotive was marvellous," said Brell. "And afterwards she said it had been one of her finest days on the Royal Train."

At Llandudno Junction, the Queen was introduced by Brell to Princess Royal Class Locomotive Trust trustees David Ward and Brian Radford along with support members Eric Riley, Mick Boothby, Barrie Wheatley, John Riley and Howard Routledge.

The train eventually left the station at 4.42pm, arriving back at Crewe around 6.15pm.

The morning footplate crew on the Duchess were Thornaby traction inspector Jim Smith, driver Graham Massey from Crewe and fireman Eddie Williamson from Crewe.

The afternoon leg saw Gareth Jones from Bescot as traction inspector, Bob Morrison from Crewe as driver and Bob Hart as fireman.

The Royal Train celebrated its 160th anniversary two days after the trip. The first time a Royal Train had been used was on June 13, 1842, when Queen Victoria travelled from Slough to Paddington on the GWR.

Brell said: "It was a magnificent performance by a very dedicated team comprising EWS, the Royal Train staff and ourselves. And I cannot praise EWS too highly for their contribution."

By contrast, there was disappointment for the 6201 Princess Elizabeth Locomotive Society, whose recently overhauled Pacific had been considered by many observers as an automatic first choice for the job if only by virtue of its name.

No. 6201 ended up being named as standby

The giant cliffside slate quarries of Penmaenmawr provide the background for the empty Royal Train working on the afternoon on June 11, 2002. PAUL BASON

Regal splendour: *Duchess of Sutherland* and its support coach head past Conwy Castle en route to Anglesey on the afternoon of June 11.
PAUL BASON

locomotive and arrived at Crewe behind an EWS Class 37 diesel on June 10. However, in view of the warm centre axle noticed during a Steamy Affairs' railtour eight days earlier, EWS ruled 'Lizzie' out of the running, and opted instead to use *Windsor Castle* to haul the Royal Train if *Sutherland* had failed.

That year, the Princess Royal Class Locomotive Trust was awarded the Heritage Railway Association's top honour, the Peter Manisty Award for Excellence, for its Royal Train feat, which had left the entire preservation movement beaming with pride.

There was widespread speculation that it was a 'one-off' and that it would be the last time steam would be used to haul a Royal Train. However, this turned out to be well wide of the mark.

THE ROYAL FIREMAN

On March 10, 2005, it was officially announced that *Duchess of Sutherland* would head another Royal Train, this time carrying Prince Charles over the Settle and Carlisle line, on Tuesday, March 22, that year.

Not only that, but Charles intended to act as fireman for part of the trip.

For the trip, the Prince donned workmen's overalls to realise every steam-era schoolboy's dream of becoming a member of a locomotive footplate crew.

Organised amid tight security for several months, the tour had its roots in an invitation by Settle resident Ruth Evans, guided walks co-ordinator for the Friends of the Settle-Carlisle Line, for the Prince to visit the famous scenic route, which was saved from closure by

Princess Royal Class Locomotive Trust chairman Brell Ewart beams with pride as he presents a replica headlamp to the Queen at Llandudno Junction. LIVERPOOL DAILY POST

The Queen arrives to reboard the steam-hauled special at Llandudno Junction.
LIVERPOOL DAILY POST

Displaying the royal headcode, *Duchess of Sutherland* waits at Holyhead at midday on June 11 for the Royal Train to be serviced. BRIAN SHARPE

The Royal Train on which Prince Charles took a turn at the shovel heads past Ais Gill on a misty March 22, 2005. FRED KERR

people power in the late Eighties.

In 2004, when the friends group was celebrating its 30th anniversary, she sent an invitation to the Prince's office at Clarence House and received a positive response.

It was so positive, in fact, that Ruth was given the task of co-ordinating the itinerary for the Prince's visit, believed to be his first trip on the Settle-Carlisle line.

On March 22, he began his visit to North Yorkshire in Clapham, where he was greeted by hundreds of flag-waving locals who lined the banks of Clapham Beck. Local couple Richard and Justina Sexton presented him with his first wedding gift from the area, a pair of rare-breed sheepskin rugs.

Afterwards, he talked to children from Clapham Primary School at the launch of the Yorkshire Dales Millennium Trust's £1 million Donate to the Dales appeal. The Prince had been patron of the appeal for seven years.

At Settle station, the Prince was met by Giggleswick and Settle Brass Band before boarding the Royal Train, which was hauled by No. 6233 for the second time.

The Royal Train leaves Valley for Llanfair PG at 9.36am on June 11, 2002. BRIAN SHARPE

Nearing the end of a memorable day: *Duchess of Sutherland* **heads towards Crewe from Chester with the Royal Train on June 11, 2002.**
JOHN SHUTTLEWORTH

At Kirkby Stephen station, the Prince was met by the trustees of the Settle and Carlisle Railway Trust, which had restored the station.

The station caretakers, retired police officer Sid Jordan and his wife Barbara, gave Charles a guided tour of their home.

He unveiled a plaque to commemorate his visit and praised representatives from the Settle and Carlisle Railway Trust for their hard work in restoring the station.

The Prince then exchanged his light grey check suit for the traditional blue overalls and black greasetop steam engineman's cap before boarding the footplate for a truly historical moment alongside EWS traction inspector Jim Smith, driver John Finlison and regular fireman Brian Grierson.

From Kirkby Stephen, he rode in the cab for the 15-minute downhill stint to Appleby.

"I can't tell you what a pleasure it is for me," the Prince said. "It really takes me back to my childhood."

He arrived at Carlisle just after 3.10pm on Platform 4 and was welcomed by two pipers from the Buccleuch and Queensferry Pipe Band.

Leaving the train, he was presented with a souvenir engraved shovel by 13-year-old Adam Miles, one of the youngest volunteers with the Princess Royal Class Locomotive Trust, which owns *Duchess of Sutherland*. Charles said that No 6233 was a "magnificent" locomotive and added: "I loved every minute of it."

He thanked support crew members Eric Riley, Barrie Wheatley and Mick Boothby, and was also introduced to trustees Brian Radford and David Ward.

Charles also spoke to Ann Turner, Virgin Trains' station manager for Carlisle. "The Prince

hoped his visit hadn't delayed the other trains," she said. "I told him that we'd just diverted them to other platforms. He said he'd enjoyed his ride and that he'd travelled at great speed."

Trust chairman Brell Ewart said: "Riding on the footplate of a crack express locomotive on the Settle to Carlisle line is the ultimate railway experience. I think the Prince enjoyed his ride on the train, especially seeing the loco at close quarters."

He briefly shook hands with cadets from the Carlisle Army Cadet Force Arnhem Company before leaving in a car for Mungrisdale to perform the official reopening of the village hall.

It was believed that the previous time that the Prince made a steam-hauled journey on the Royal Train was on August 10, 1962, when he went to begin his first term at Gordonstoun School in Scotland. ∎

No. 6233 heads the Royal Train carrying the Queen and Duke of Edinburgh across Anglesey at Rhosneigr on June 11, 2002. JOHN SHUTTLEWORTH

CHAPTER TEN

RESTREAMLINING A DUCHESS

A sight not seen for 60 years: restreamlined Princess Coronation Pacific No. 6229 *Duchess of Hamilton* as unveiled in the Great Hall at the National Railway Museum on May 20, 2009. ROBIN JONES

The sight of streamlined Princess Coronation Pacifics predated the volunteer-led preservation movement.

All the casings had been removed by 1949, with only No. 46243 *City of Lancaster* carrying its British Railways number while streamlined.

In 1951, the Talyllyn Railway became the first in the world to be taken over and operated by enthusiasts.

From small acorns, a forest of mighty oaks flourished, and many miracles were performed by the preservation sector.

The creation of the Ffestiniog Railway's deviation around the Llyn Ystradau reservoir with its double spiral; the restoration of unique BR 8P Pacific No. 71000 *Duke of Gloucester* from partially cut Barry scrapyard condition and the honing of its main line performance to perfection (which British Railways had failed to achieve); the creation of the world's first double track heritage trunk line in the form of the Great Central Railway at Loughborough; and the building from scratch of a new LNER main line Pacific locomotive in the form of A1 Peppercorn Pacific No. 60163 *Tornado* are some that spring immediately to mind, but there are many others.

Often, the aim is to re-create a major aspect of railway heritage that is glaringly missing from the preservation portfolio.

In 1998, coming firmly into this category was the absence of a streamlined Princess Coronation Pacific.

The heritage sector had inherited three Duchesses, two of which had originally been streamlined. To re-create one in its original form, the obvious solution – far cheaper than building a new locomotive – was to back-convert an existing one.

During 1998, talks between the National Railway Museum and Steve McColl, production director of luxury train operator Venice-Simplon Orient Express and former head of British Rail's Special Trains Unit, about rebuilding *Duchess of Hamilton* in its original form and returning it to the main line were conducted.

At a meeting of the Friends of the National Railway Museum's 229 Club, the locomotive's supporters' association, at York on September 12, an agreement was announced.

A ground-breaking deal had been struck whereby *Duchess of Hamilton* in its original condition would become the principal steam locomotive for a new north of England luxury charter train to be launched in 2000 by VSOE.

In return for covering the estimated £300,000 cost of the overhaul, VSOE would be able to use No. 6229 for up to 30 main line trips each year during the period of its seven-year boiler ticket. The locomotive would also be made available for other enthusiast charters and, where time permitted, visits to heritage lines, and when not in use could be displayed at the museum itself.

It was intended that VSOE would take on responsibility for the rebuild, with the NRM providing a detailed specification.

Much of the rebuild was to take place at the York museum itself, but the overhaul of the boiler and the manufacture of the streamlined casing to replace the one removed in 1947 would be undertaken by subcontractors.

Air braking and a spark arrestor which would allow the rebuilt No. 6229 to operate during the peak summer periods during times of high fire risk would be installed.

The museum wanted to see No. 6229 reappear in its original LMS crimson lake livery with gold bands, while VSOE instead wanted it to be painted in LMS blue with silver stripes –

A classic line-up of Crewe-built Class 8 LMS/London Midland Region Pacifics at the September 10-11, 2005, *Heritage Railway*-sponsored Crewe Works Great Gathering open weekend. From left are: No. 71000 *Duke of Gloucester*, No. 6233 *Duchess of Sutherland*, sister No. 46229 *Duchess of Hamilton*, No. 46203 *Princess Margaret Rose* and No. 6201 *Princess Elizabeth*. FRED KERR

for it intended to complete a 10- or 12-coach matching train in that livery.

VSOE had just taken over Regency Rail Cruises and its fleet of five main line-registered coaches and also taken delivery of Mk.1 and Mk.2 coaches from rolling stock hire company Rail Charter Services. It was intended that these vehicles would be refurbished by restoration company LNWR Co Ltd, then owned by founder and pop music mogul Pete Waterman, at Crewe, and reliveried in LMS corporate blue.

A pair of six-wheel milk wagons passed for 75mph running would carry extra water for the streamlined Duchess, which would be running on a network where much of the steam era infrastructure including water columns had been ripped out. Class 50 diesel No. 50008 *Thunderer* would also be present in the new luxury train to provide power for heating and air conditioning, as well as acting as a standby in the event of the Duchess failing, and would be painted in the same livery.

Overall, the restreamlining scheme received a rapturous reception from the enthusiast fraternity.

The locomotive was dismantled in the museum's new workshop, and a subsequent investigation of the boiler revealed no major problems to prevent its restoration in line with original estimates made by the National

No.46229 *Duchess of Hamilton* in British Railways maroon livery with 1956 emblem at the National Railway Museum in August 2001. HUGH LLEWELLYN*

Railway Museum's head of engineering collections Richard Gibbon.

All that was needed was final ratification by the VSOE board on receipt of the inspection report.

However, months went by and no final decision by the train operator was

forthcoming. In late 1999, it was announced that the decision had been placed "on hold", especially in the light of renewed fears about the future of main line steam.

On October 5, 1999, 31 people were killed and more than 520 injured in the Ladbroke Grove rail crash, the worst rail accident on the

Tyseley's chief mechanical engineer Bob Meanley (left) oversees the trial fitting of the first parts of the streamlined casing. NRM

Casing panels being machined at Tyseley. NRM

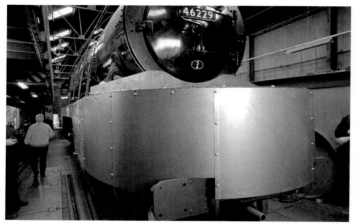

The streamlined casing around the front buffer beam and the platform which will support the two front doors of the housing, as seen on May 26, 2007. ROBIN JONES

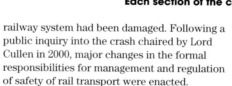

Each section of the casing had to be made by hand. NRM

Great Western Main Line. It was said that, as with the nearby Southall rail crash of September 1997, it would have been prevented by an operational Automatic Train Protection, but wider fitting of this had been rejected on cost grounds.

Public confidence in the management and regulation of safety of Britain's privatised railway system had been damaged. Following a public inquiry into the crash chaired by Lord Cullen in 2000, major changes in the formal responsibilities for management and regulation of safety of rail transport were enacted.

VSOE feared that had main line steam been curtailed and the use of a restreamlined Duchess restricted, the rebuild might not be cost effective.

At the same time, VSOE cancelled its northern Regency Rail Land Cruise operation pending a spring relaunch.

However, at the end of February 2000, Steve McColl, a former general manager of the East Somerset Railway, suddenly parted company with VSOE.

Richard Gibbon wrote to VSOE to ask what its intentions were for the streamlining project in view of its main protagonist's departure. VSOE had given the end of February as a deadline for its decision, but none was forthcoming.

Museum officials realised that the project was dead in the water and made arrangements to reassemble No. 46229 as a static exhibit, in its rebuilt form.

On October 5, 2001, Steve McColl was sentenced to nine months' imprisonment by Chester Crown Court after pleading guilty to obtaining £27,150 by fraud from VSOE. The money had been obtained for design work on a Class 50 diesel and several coaches which was not done, and one of the vehicles did not even exist, the court was told.

There were, however, others who still dreamed of seeing a Duchess running in its original condition.

In early 2002, Bury locomotive engineer and owner Ian Riley asked the museum if he could restore Duchess of Hamilton to its original streamlined condition for main line running.

The thinness of the streamlined casing is apparent in this view of the section covering the left-hand piston. ROBIN JONES

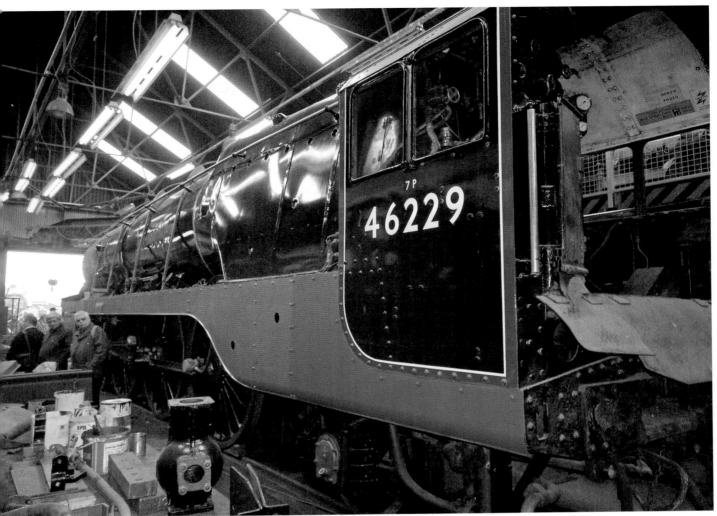

A transformation in place from floor level upwards: No. 46229 reverts to No. 6229. ROBIN JONES

Ian was looking for a 'big name' locomotive to spearhead his own train operating company which at the time he was planning to set up. He also asked about the availability of BR Britannia Pacific No. 70013 *Oliver Cromwell*, which at the time was on "permanent loan" to Bressingham Steam Museum in Norfolk.

However, the subsequent talks came to nothing.

THIRD TIME LUCKY

In 2004, the museum announced that it was to spend £70,000 on a fresh study into the feasibility of restreamlining No. 46229, in partnership with the Friends of the NRM's 229 Club and Tyseley Locomotive Works in south Birmingham.

A museum spokesman enthused: "This is a unique project not only because of the nature of the task, but also because many of the skills used in Crewe works to complete the locomotive will have been lost and the study will seek to rediscover exactly how the streamlining was constructed and applied to the locomotive. This is also the condition in which the engine toured the United States before the outbreak of the Second World War."

The study considered the level of the work required to restreamline the engine to the original specification, that is to full main line standard. While it was being undertaken, the Duchess remained on static display in the

Great Hall at York alongside LNER streamliner and world steam record holder *Mallard*.

The project was to be led by Donald Heath after the 229 Club unanimously approved the scheme, while overviewing its management and future certification matters was to be club member Graeme Bunker; and father-and-son team Bob and Alastair Meanley from Tyseley Locomotive Works would oversee engineering.

The following year, *Duchess of Hamilton* was booked to appear as a static exhibit at the Great Gathering – Crewe Works Festival of Rail open weekend on September 10-11, an event sponsored by *Heritage Railway* magazine. On August 22, 2005, it was moved from the Great Hall into the adjacent workshop to undergo preparatory work before travelling to Crewe. In order to facilitate the move, the locomotive was subjected to ultrasonic axle testing, eddy-current testing and an underkeep examination, while pistons and crossheads were stripped.

After the event, it was hauled by the West Coast Railway Company's Class 37 No. 37197 via the West Coast Main Line to Tyseley, where the feasibility study was completed. The findings proved favourable and the museum gave the green light for the restreamlining to take place there.

A nationwide appeal was launched to fund the restreamlining project, and raised around £30,000, to which the Friends of the NRM added another £60,000.

The casing in place inside Tyseley Locomotive Works on January 21, 2009. ROBIN JONES

The streamlined tender with fins fitted at the rear. ROBIN JONES

The original 1938 colour panel from 1937 reunited with the locomotive at Tyseley on May 26, 2007, to ensure the correct paint match. ROBIN JONES

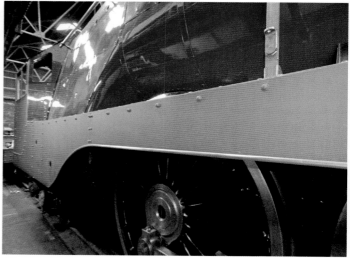

The streamlined curves begin to take shape again. ROBIN JONES

However, it became clear that another £20,000 was needed. Tyseley's chief mechanical engineer Bob Meanley opted to bring in an outside contractor to bend the metal sheet to construct the front doors of the casing because of their extremely complex geometrical shape.

Previous schemes to restreamline the locomotive had highlighted this as the most intricate and difficult part of the task. Fortunately this time round the engineers came across an archive image of *Duchess of Hamilton* showing the front doors of the streamlined casing wide open. The image was then blown up to such a scale that almost every detail could be seen.

The museum's then curator of rail vehicles Jim Rees said: "We know for a fact that the engineers who originally streamlined *Duchess of Hamilton* had problems with the compound curves of the doors – and we have too.

"The doors of the *Duchess of Hamilton*'s streamlining hinge on different pivot points so that they open upwards as well as out. The best way to describe it would be to imagine the way a ladybird's wings open just before it's about to fly."

Andy Bassnett, a blacksmith based in Malton, North Yorkshire, had a perfect understanding of the compound curve of the double doors and was able to hand-make the frames to perfection.

THE RIGHT COLOUR

The three surviving Princess Coronation Pacifics 'came together' in Birmingham on Saturday, May 26, 2007.

No 6233 *Duchess of Sutherland* passed through the city with the Princess Margaret Rose Tours 'Oxfordshire Express' which was steam hauled from Derby to Didcot.

It came within whistling distance of both No. 46235 *City of Birmingham*, a static exhibit inside the city centre's Thinktank museum, and No. 46229 *Duchess of Hamilton*, being retro-converted to its original streamlined form at Tyseley.

There, members of the 229 Club gathered two hours after *Sutherland* had passed

The streamlined casing reaching to the smokebox; all that is now needed are the double front doors. ROBIN JONES

The casing sheet is fitted over the left-hand piston. ROBIN JONES

through Tyseley station to view the work on fitting the new streamlined casing to No. 46229 completed to date. Supporters were able to walk around the locomotive inside the works and view the streamlined casing fitted to date to the locomotive beneath footplate level. Also on display was the tender, which had already been fully streamlined.

Bob Meanley announced that paint manufacturer John Scanlon of Weston-super-Mare had agreed to supply the paint for the project free of charge, and matching it to the exact shade of the original LMS crimson with gold lining would take place in coming weeks.

Paint changes colour over time, so there was no easy way of knowing exactly what shade of LMS red or maroon *Duchess of Hamilton* was painted in when it was outshopped in 1938.

Luckily, the man who had been brought in to paint the locomotive, Bob Timmins, had taken part in a debate over the colour of 'LMS red' back in the Sixties. During the debate he met a man who had a barrel of LMS red dried powder pigment.

This man gave Bob Timmins a bag of the pigment – which afterwards remained perfectly preserved in the darkness of his attic for more than 40 years.

Jim Rees said: "LMS red has been the 'holy grail' for many engineers and railway enthusiasts for years, so to actually have discovered the exact shade as a result of this project is a fantastic by-product that none of us could have anticipated."

At the preview, Bob Meanley said that another £15,000 was needed to complete the streamlined casing – which was being built to conform to the lower modern main line clearances, all ready for any future steaming. However, the current project did not include the locomotive returning to steam, but only for static display in York.

ABOVE: In early 2011, the National Railway Museum's then director Steve Davies raised the possibility of a future return of *Duchess of Hamilton* to steam and the national network. In the meantime, for static display purposes, the museum repainted one of its LMS coaches, a corridor third-class brake, into streamlined LMS crimson lake with gold speed lines to match No. 6229. Repair work to the roof was also undertaken. The locomotive and coach pair were unveiled at the York museum's September 24-25 steam weekend. Museum rail operations co-ordinator said: "*Duchess of Hamilton* is one of our most popular exhibits in its streamlined form and the museum saw it as the perfect opportunity to make the display even more eye-catching by pairing it with a matching coach." NRM

Machining a curved panel for the front casing double doors. NRM

The double doors take shape around the jig. NRM

The jig around which the double doors, the most difficult part of the streamlining, were shaped. NRM

Shaping a curved panel for the front doors. NRM

Fitting another piece of the double doors jigsaw. NRM

Smoothing the curved edges of the double doors. NRM

Welding the panels into position. NRM

A WORLDWIDE SEARCH FOR STEEL

At Tyseley, *Duchess of Hamilton* was fitted with a new tapered smokebox to accommodate the casing and displayed as a 'semi', one side of the locomotive having been painted in LMS black livery.

Before the streamlined casing could be formed, the correct steel had to be found.

However, it was soon discovered that the large sheets of steel necessary to make the casing – needing to be just the right thickness so it could be bent into the correct shape – were no longer as readily available as they once were. A worldwide search for the correct steel resulted in a year-long stalling of the project.

A year into the search, Corus, Europe's

Jean Shuttleworth rode on the 'Coronation' from London to Glasgow behind a streamlined Duchess in 1938 – and 71 years later, on the evening of May 20, 2009, was a guest at the relaunch of the restreamlined No 6229 after her son, West Coast Railways commercial manager James Shuttleworth, helped bring it from Tyseley to York. ROBIN JONES

second largest steel producer, was able to roll steel of the correct size and thickness especially for the project.

Several sheets of the 1.5mm steel sheet were obtained with the aid of Prime Minister Gordon Brown's office.

Furthermore, the locomotive's cab was found to be out of position and needed rectification work.

However, all the work done was compatible with it being returned to the main line at a time when sufficient funds were available.

Many 229 Club members turned up to inspect the latest progress on the project at Tyseley at another private event on January 21, 2009.

The casing had been installed around the middle of the boiler. However, the double doors, the most difficult part of the casing to build, had not yet been fitted.

UNVEILED AT LAST!

Finally, the Duchess was returned to the York museum on May 18, 2009, behind a West Coast Railways Class 47 diesel ready for its high-profile public relaunch.

That took place two days later on the evening of May 20, and it did not disappoint for one second.

On that day, a fabled shape from the distant zenith of the steam age reappeared in the public gaze to widespread acclaim, following the completion of this unique project which spanned four years.

Many enthusiasts had initially expressed lukewarm feelings about plans to restore preservation icon Princess Coronation Pacific *Duchess of Hamilton* to its as-built 1938 condition, with air-smoothed streamlined casing.

The left-hand cabside with the gold numerals. ROBIN JONES

Classic images of halcyon times: the art deco design of *Duchess of Hamilton* is mirrored by the curves of this fabulous Chrysler Airflow C1 from 1935, which was displayed alongside the Stanier masterpiece during and after its relaunch at the National Railway Museum. The Airflow was one of the first full-size American production cars to use streamlining as a basis for building a sleeker automobile, one less susceptible to air resistance. Chrysler made a significant effort at a fundamental change in automotive design with the model, but despite its striking art deco appearance, it was ultimately a huge commercial failure. ROBIN JONES

In Thirties style, the New York Jazz Band celebrates the unveiling of the restreamlined Duchess in the Great Hall at the National Railway Museum on May 20, 2009. ROBIN JONES

Eye for detail: the headlamps are art deco too! ROBIN JONES

The brand-new casing as viewed from the rear. ROBIN JONES

Any lingering doubts about the controversial decision by the Friends of the National Railway Museum's 229 Club to restore Hamilton to its original form were dispelled within seconds as it made its debut in the Great Hall.

The verdict from around 300 VIPs and invited guests who were present to witness the long-awaited occasion was – it is simply magnificent.

The 'reborn' No. 6229 immediately took pride of place in a new free exhibition – Streamlined: Styling An Era – which explored the links between 1930s society, engineering and art deco design using the Duchess as the central exhibit.

Museum display content manager Joe Savage said: "The subject matter is particularly topical in the current economic climate, as the 1930s was also a time of world recession when companies were struggling to sell their products.

"Against this background, a new generation of young designers began adopting styles devised as experiments for scientific streamlining and applying them to consumer products such as fridges and cameras to turn them into objects of desire.

"*Duchess of Hamilton* is a stunning example of art deco opulence, which when it was built in 1938 wowed design critics on both sides of the Atlantic. Its streamlined look was symbolic of the trend which became the icon of an era.

Valances over the left-hand wheel arch. ROBIN JONES

The National Collection's LMS Corridor Brake Third No. 5987 as repainted in crimson lake livery with gold speed lines to match *Duchess of Hamilton,* and now permanently displayed behind the iconic locomotive in the Great Hall of the National Railway Museum. ROBIN JONES

"It is one of the most significant products of the streamline era. Its streamlined form embodied the language of speed and sold an exciting image of modernity to potential passengers.

"During a time of hardship, the streamlined shape turned *Duchess of Hamilton* into an exciting symbol of progress and now, even in the current economic climate, it still has the power to inspire."

Jim Rees described another problem that had been tackled by the project's engineers.

"My favourite thing that indicates the accuracy of this project is the fact that Tyseley broke dozens of quarter inch drill bits," he said.

"When all the streamlining was taken off Duchess, it left lots of holes in the platework which needed to be welded up to leave a flat plate again.

"Because Tyseley followed some of the original drawings so accurately – and the original streamlining was fitted so accurately

to the drawings – the engineers at Tyseley drilled through the exact same points that were originally drilled into and then welded back up again.

"It is a lot more difficult to drill through a weld than normal steel so Tyseley has gone through dozens of quarter inch drill bits to get the job done.

Concluded Jim: "Those broken drills bits are the evidence of exactly how accurate this job is,". ∎

Back on the national network: *Duchess of Hamilton,* back in its original 1938 as-built form, is taken on the main line from Tyseley to York behind a Class 47 diesel on May 19. DAVID DEPPER

Bob Meanley, chief mechanical engineer at Tyseley Locomotive Works, who masterminded the implementation of the restreamlining project including the delicate re-creation of the casing's front double doors. ROBIN JONES

CHAPTER ELEVEN

THE BLACK DUCHESS

Pride of the Princess Royal Class Locomotive Trust fleet: ex-Butlins pair Nos. 6233 *Duchess of Sutherland* and No. 46203 *Princess Margaret Rose* outside the West Shed on March 16, 2010. ROBIN JONES

Crimson lake no more: under a leaden sky, No. 6233 *Duchess of Sutherland* displays its somewhat sombre postwar LMS lined black livery alongside West Shed stablemate Princess Royal Pacific No. 46203 *Princess Margaret Rose* on March 6. ROBIN JONES

Both before and after its exploits on the Royal Train, *Duchess of Sutherland* built up a sizeable following among the British enthusiast fraternity, filling the void left by the withdrawal of *Duchess of Hamilton*.

However, often in the next breath following expressions of admiration, many a linesider voiced the view that it should not be painted in LMS crimson lake, as built new with a single chimney and no smoke deflectors, but in the 'more authentic' Brunswick green that British Railways adopted from Stanier's old employer the GWR.

Indeed, it carried BR green livery from November 29, 1952, until its withdrawal, the appearance best remembered by the armies of Fifties and early Sixties schoolboy trainspotters, many of whom evolved into preservationists.

The Princess Royal Class Locomotive Trust, however, would hear none of it. No. 6233 was designed and built by the LMS and should therefore represent that company's corporate colours in preservation, it was persistently decreed by the owning group.

However, on March 6, 2010, No. 6233 was rolled out of the West Shed in none other than LMS lined black livery.

It was not the first time that the locomotive had been painted black. The Ivatt intermediate black livery had been carried from October 28, 1947, until May 19, 1950, when it emerged in British Railways Caledonian blue, a short-lived livery applied to express passenger locomotives.

The trustees had wavered in this insistence that No. 6233 carry the crimson lake livery that had by then become its heritage era trademark.

By 2010, it needed a new coat of paintwork, but its 10-year overhaul was due within a year

A 1946 LMS poster based on a Terence Cuneo painting illustrating a black Duchess being turned inside a depot.

despite it having been granted an extension.

Rather than run up the cost of a new coat of crimson lake, the trustees opted for cheaper but authentic Ivatt lined black livery.

It was not what the enthusiast following had hoped for, but it rang the changes and proved popular.

Its short-lived spell in black ended on a flourish, with three trips in 15 days before the

final curtain descended.

The first of the three trains, the Carlisle-Stirling 'Royal Scot' on Saturday, October 2, 2010, produced something of a mixed bag in terms of overall performance on the day.

The train, diesel hauled from Stafford, arrived at Carlisle nine minutes down, but a quick change of motive power enabled departure to be made a minute over right time.

The sleek lines of a Duchess are just as magnificent in black as any other colour. ROBIN JONES

On its first main line run in LMS black livery, No. 6233 *Duchess of Sutherland* passes Toton depot with Princess Margaret Rose Tours' 'Yorkshire Coronation' to Scarborough on April 10. 2010. KEN WOOLLEY

Duchess of Sutherland accelerates away from Preston just south of Euxton Junction with PMR Tours' 'Citadel Express' returning from Carlisle to Crewe on May 8, 2010. FRED KERR

In a tightly timed schedule, following signal checks en route and some might say excessive regulation, the 'Scot' was reported as 30 minutes down arriving at Stirling, none of it booked to the engine.

On the return journey, similar checks amounted to a total of 20 minutes lost yet a spirited attack south bound on Shap not only won the 4-6-2 a new record for the climb, but also reduced the arrears to 10 minutes when arriving at Carnforth.

It was here it was noticed that the leading crank axle wheelset had run a hotbox. With the second of the three trains booked for the following Saturday, speedy reaction was required to enable the 4-6-2 to pass its fitness to run exam by the end of the following week.

Quick action there was. The wheelset having been dropped, arrangements were made for despatch by road to Tyseley for skimming. Departing from Carnforth on the Monday morning, the carrier reached Tyseley that evening.

In an outstanding effort, chief engineer Bob Meanley organised his team to use the whole of Tuesday to skim and polish the injured journal. They did. On Wednesday, the wheelset was back on the road heading for Carnforth, arriving late afternoon.

Meanwhile, West Coast engineers, led by John Haddow, had remetalled the axlebox and by Thursday had repositioned the wheelset and made the 4-6-2 ready for the road, the Duchess departing for Southall at 10am.

Thanks to the efforts of all concerned the 4-6-2 was prepped for its next trip, a Euston-Chester 'Cathedrals Express' departing on Saturday, October 9, taking Camden bank and the ensuing 31 miles of rising gradients to Tring in its stride despite a load of 13 full coaches behind the drawbar.

Showing its style, the shiny black engine rolled its train into Chester one minute early.

A similar well-judged performance on the return journey was spoiled by signal checks at

No. 6233 storms past Ais Gill with a Carlisle to Liverpool Lime Street working on August 21, 2010. FRED KERR

No. 6233 arrives at Euston from Chester with Steam Dreams' 'Cathedrals Express' on October 9, 2010. DON BENN

Duchess of Sutherland is seen just south of Birkett Tunnel heading the Railway Touring Company's 'Cumbrian Mountain Express' from Carlisle on August 28, 2010. PETER AINSWORTH

Northampton, Milton Keynes, and approaching the north Wembley area meant that the train arrived at Euston 10 minutes adrift of booked time.

It was the first time that a Stanier Coronation 4-6-2 had worked out of Euston since 2004 and the first time that one had worked into Euston since 1963.

The Duchess completed its third and final trip on October 16, heading the 'London Explorer', diesel hauled from Sheffield to Derby where No. 6233 took charge for the onward journey via Nottingham and Grantham to King's Cross, a Stanier engine working over the LNER's high speed main line.

The October 16 trip marked the last trip on a Duchess for one of the best-known heritage era enginemen, Bill Andrew, who was also believed to be the UK's longest-serving railwayman, and who retired two months later at the age of 75.

He began his footplate career with British Railways as a 15-year-old cleaner at Rose Grove in 1950, and often acted a fireman to his uncle, Ernest Whittaker.

In 1956, he moved to Crewe North and rose up through the ranks to achieve senior No. 1 link, remaining at Crewe for the rest of his career.

He later became an instructor on class 50 diesels and the Advanced Passenger Train.

Having served as West Coast Railways' traction inspector since 2000, Bill was on the footplate of *Duchess of Sutherland*. ∎

Bill Andrew at King's Cross on the footplate of *Duchess of Sutherland* on October 16, 2010. Behind is Malcolm Baker, chairman of the 6233 Trust. This was Bill's last turn on the main line with a Duchess. PHIL MARSH

Duchess of Sutherland stands at Derby after arriving from King's Cross on Saturday, October 16, with its final railtour before withdrawal for **overhaul.** RALF EDGE

CHAPTER TWELVE

SUTHERLAND TURNS GREEN!

Turning green: No. 46233 *Duchess of Sutherland* in steam outside its West Shed home on November 29, 2011. BARRY COLMAN

No. 46233 returned to the main line in its new green livery on March 29, 2012. It is seen accelerating away from Derby past Peartree with a PMR Tours 'Night Owl' proving run to Crewe. BRIAN SHARPE

It's 1952 all over again, as No. 46233 raises a head of steam on March 3, 2012. ROBIN JONES

For years, it seemed that the trustees of the Princess Royal Class Locomotive Trust would not be budged.

The edict of the owning group was that No. 6233 *Duchess of Sutherland* would remain in LMS crimson lake in perpetuity, despite the temporary 'lapse' into Ivatt black.

However, after the boiler ticket of No. 6233 expired in November 2010, it seemed there was a change of heart.

The following year, the trust unveiled a novel new way of raising money towards the overhaul and repaint.

The public would be invited to vote for their choice of livery – at £1 a time via the trust's website, or £1.50 a time by ringing a choice of premium-rate telephone numbers from a BT landline.

Each telephone line was dedicated to a separate colour choice.

The winning livery would be carried for a year, after which *Duchess of Sutherland* would revert to LMS crimson lake.

That was considered long enough for those passionate about another colour to have their fill and provide numerous chances for lineside photographers before No. 6233 reverted to its trademark livery.

The trust offered the options of LMS crimson lake, BR green, BR blue and LMS black. It was decided not to go for BR maroon, an option previously considered by the trust as a "halfway house" because it would split the LMS crimson lake vote.

There was no limit placed on the number of votes per person. If anyone wished to vote 10 or more times, a form could be downloaded from the trust website, avoiding large

Still with a few finishing touches required at the front end, and with deflectors and nameplates still to be fitted, No. 46233 *Duchess of Sutherland* passes Swanwick Junction during mileage accumulation trips at the Midland Railway-Butterley on January 7, 2012.
BRIAN SHARPE

telephone charges.

A running total of the votes was updated and published each Sunday afternoon on the trust's website.

The Race for the Livery had the enthusiast fraternity gripped for several months, until the telephone lines closed at 11.59pm on Wednesday, August 31, 2011.

Would a well-to-do enthusiast buy hundreds of votes at the last minute to get his or her choice of livery? The speculation mounted.

Finally, the results were announced on September 4. A total of 51% – 3802 – had voted for Brunswick green, as opposed to just 31% – 2346 – for another spell of LMS crimson lake.

Just 15% – 1123 – wanted BR express

The latest overhaul of No. 6233 rapidly entering its final stages in the West Shed on November 25, 2011. Notice the first coat of green paint on the end of the tender!
DEREK HOSKINS*

The one that so many people had been waiting for, or thought they would never see: green-liveried No. 46233 *Duchess of Sutherland* carrying a 'Royal Scot' headboard unveiled at its West Shed home on March 3, 2012. ROBIN JONES

Duchess of Sutherland heads between Penmaenmawr and Conwy with Steam Dreams' 'Cathedrals Express' from Holyhead on **September 20.** MYLES JONES

With the castle in the background. No. 46233 accelerates from Stirling past Bannockburn with PMR Tours' 'Caledonian' returning to Wolverhampton with steam haulage as far as Carlisle on October 6. PHIL WATERFIELD

passenger blue, and only 3% – 188 voters – wanted LMS black again.

The trust was true to its word.

Reassembly of the 4-6-2 made steady progress after the boiler passed its hydraulic and steam tests, the latter at Crewe on October 3, 2011.

Events moved swiftly after that, the boiler being lifted back into the frames on October 17 and the cab refitted on October 21.

By the end of that month, cladding had been completed and the engine's nameplates fitted into position.

At the beginning of November, preparation work for painting was started while other work continued on schedule.

Having only been reunited with its newly overhauled boiler a month earlier, *Duchess of Sutherland* was to be seen raising steam outside the West Shed at the Midland Railway-Butterley on November 29.

It was the first time in preservation that the locomotive had carried its British Railways identity, with the 46233 numberplate fixed to the smokebox.

The first steps towards its repaint into Brunswick green livery – reviled by some LMS aficionados because it had been adopted by British Railways from Big Four rival the Great Western – had also been taken, with the cab and tender sides in dark green undercoat.

No. 46233 made its first moves under its own steam during the following week.

Finally, on March 3, 2012, the wishes of many enthusiasts were fulfilled with the official unveiling of the locomotive in BR green for the second time in its history.

As early-morning drizzle gave way to

A second green Duchess in preservation: No. 46233 minus the headboard at its launch.
ROBIN JONES

Duchess of Sutherland calls at Carlisle on the Glasgow-Preston leg of the Railway Touring Company's 'Great Britain V' tour on April 26, **2012.** DAVE RODGERS

No. 46233 *Duchess of Sutherland* **storms up Shap with the Railway Touring Company's 'Scottish Lowlander' on September 27, 2014.**
HENRY ELLIOTT

Duchess of Sutherland *having arrived at Euston with PMR Tours' 'London Explorer' from Derby on October 20, 2012.* JOHN TITLOW

sunshine, the completed locomotive was officially rolled out of its West Shed home at the Midland Railway-Butterley as a crowd of admiring photographers gathered.

The locomotive ran up and down the shed yard, carrying a 'Royal Scot' headboard which was later removed.

GREEN PARTY IN FULL SWING

On April 21 that year, No. 46233 became what is believed to be the first green Duchess to appear at York station, hauling its first full-scale railtour from Derby to Scarborough and back for PMR Tours.

Green Duchesses had been seen at Leeds (No. 46255 on a railtour) and Newcastle on diversions in the early Fifties, but only red-liveried No. 46229 *Duchess of Hamilton* and No. 6233 are believed to have run through York. When No. 6256 *Sir William A. Stanier F.R.S.* went through York during the 1948 locomotive exchanges, it was in LMS black livery.

Later that day, LNER A4 streamlined Pacific No. 4464 *Bittern*, a member of the class that came closest to rivalling the Princess Coronations, arrived with a railtour.

On May 26, 2012, *Duchess of Sutherland* again tackled Shap. Not since 1964 had a green-liveried Duchess been seen tackling the climb through the Westmorland Fells.

Bound for Shap and Carlisle, No. 46233 accelerates away from Crewe with PMR Tours' 'Citadel Express' on May 26, 2012. DICK MANTON

As attention was focused on the National Railway Museum's phenomenally-successful events held to mark the 75th anniversary of A4 streamlined Pacific No. 4468 *Mallard*'s 126mph world speed record run, *Duchess of Sutherland* was celebrating its 75th birthday, having emerged from Crewe Works in July 1938.

The Princess Royal Class Locomotive Trust ran a special 600-mile anniversary tour over two days, September 6-7, from Sheffield to Perth, again taking in Shap, with No. 46233 coming on at Crewe.

A gala dinner was held at the Station Hotel in Perth on the evening of September 6.

A NEW STREET FIRST

Duchess of Sutherland made history once more on Saturday, June 28, 2014, when it headed Vintage Trains' 'The Midlander' from New Street to Euston nonstop.

It was the first time that a Duchess had run out of New Street to London since the class was withdrawn in 1964.

Tyseley Locomotive Works chief engineer Bob Meanly has praised Network Rail planners for finding a way to operate steam specials from Birmingham to New Street much more easily.

Lack of platform space at the station, which is currently under redevelopment, has led to a situation where there was limited scope for a diesel on the end of the train to decouple and run round.

However, route planners at Network Rail's Milton Keynes office found a solution.

The answer was to reroute steam specials north out of New Street, and on to the Grand Junction line and Soho loop in order to turn round and face the right way to London from Stechford onwards.

Duchess of Sutherland passes Mossley on the climb to Standedge with the Railway Touring Company's first 'Scarborough Flyer' from Crewe, on July 26, 2013. DICK MANTON

No. 46233 made a very rare visit to another heritage line when it starred in the Mid-Norfolk Railway's summer steam gala in 2013. It is seen accelerating away from Kimberley Park with air-braked Mk.2 coaching stock on July 19. BRIAN SHARPE

On June 29, 2013, No. 46233 arrives at York with Vintage Trains 'Scarborough Flyer' from Tyseley Warwick Road, the Duchess coming on at Derby. ROBIN JONES

In the summer of 2013, No. 46233 *Duchess of Sutherland* celebrated its 75th anniversary. PMR Tours' September 7 anniversary trip, returning from Perth to Crewe, brought it shoulder to shoulder with another of its great rivals, LNER A4 Pacific No. 60009 *Union of South Africa* at Carlisle Citadel. DAVID TROUT

THE FAREWELL TRIP RERUN

On September 27, 2014, 50 years and one day since the last British Railways service hauled by a Duchess, the Railway Touring Company repeated the 'Scottish Lowlander' railtour from that day.

Of course, No. 46256 *Sir William A. Stanier F.R.S.*, which had been retained in traffic for a final two weeks after other class members were withdrawn, was not available this time round, as it had been scrapped a few weeks later – but No. 46233 stepped into the breach.

The 1964 tour, organised by the Lancashire and North West branch of the Railway Correspondence & Travel Society, also included A4 Pacifics Nos. 60007 *Sir Nigel Gresley* and No. 60009 *Union of South Africa* and ran from Crewe to Carlisle, Edinburgh, Glasgow, Carlisle and Crewe to mark the end of Stanier Pacifics.

The 2014 tour, which ran from Crewe to Edinburgh and back, with No. 46233 coming off at Carlisle, also saw No. 60009 once again operate the Scottish portion of the tour.

In the support coach was Bill Ashcroft, who had organised the 1964 tour, and fireman Brian Fare who had been on the footplate of No. 46256.

Shap was conquered at a modest 27mph. Before the trip, it had been discovered that there was a faulty bearing on No. 46233's centre driving axle, but it was given the green light to take part on the condition that there would be no continuous 75mph running.

On the way back, No. 46233 took over from the A4 at Carlisle, the two engines posing side by side during the changeover, as happened in 1964.

At one stage, the train reached 60mph, and maintained a speed in excess of 50mph all the way to Shap. However, the Duchess was taken off in Carnforth loop, to be replaced by West Coast Railways' Jubilee 4-6-0 No.45699 *Galatea* back to Crewe.

Those who voted for BR green got more than they bargained for. In summer 2014, the Princess Royal Class Locomotive Trust announced that No. 46233 would be staying in the popular livery until July 2015.

The extension came about after the trust decided to postpone its planned winter maintenance.

When the maintenance is carried out, the Duchess will again become LMS No. 6233 in crimson lake – unless there is another sudden change of heart. ■

The green Duchess crosses Oxford Road bridge in Manchester. DEREK PHILLIPS

LMS Princess Coronation Pacific No. 46233 *Duchess of Sutherland* **crosses the Forth Bridge with a Scottish Railway Preservation Society 'Forth Circle' working on September 14, 2014.** DEREK PHILLIPS

No. 46233 *Duchess of Sutherland* **waits to depart Euston with Vintage Trains' 'The Midlander' which had arrived non-stop from Birmingham New Street on June 28, 2014.** JOHN TITLOW

CHAPTER THIRTEEN

CITY OF BIRMINGHAM:
the third Duchess

To celebrate the 75th anniversary of *Mallard*'s world speed record run on Stoke bank in Lincolnshire on July 3, 1938, the National Railway Museum organised a reunion of all six of the surviving streamlined A4 Pacifics.

The idea of former museum director Steve Davies, the celebration would involve the temporary repatriation of exiles No. 60008 *Dwight D. Eisenhower* from the US National Railroad Museum at Green Bay in Wisconsin, and No. 60010 *Dominion of Canada* from the Canadian equivalent, the Exporail museum in Montreal.

Mission impossible? Since the pair were exported across the Atlantic in the Sixties, having been saved from the scrapyard and given new permanent homes primarily because

of their names, there had been several inquiries and offers to bring them back, but all had been firmly rebuffed by their museum owners.

Steve, however, had a different idea. Both locomotives were showing their age in terms of bodywork, and in return for borrowing them for up to two years for the Mallard 75 event, they would be cosmetically restored.

An agreement was reached, and West Midlands-based haulier Moveright International completed an epic journey across North America and the Atlantic to bring them back to Liverpool.

No. 60008 was refurbished in its Brunswick Green identity, while No. 60010 was returned to its as-built condition as No. 4489 in garter blue, complete with the ceremonial bell which it had been given by the Canadian government when it was brand new.

At three Great Gatherings held to mark *Mallard* 75 year, two at the National Railway Museum in York in 2013 and the last at its Locomotion outreach station in Shildon, the pair were reunited with the four UK survivors, No. 60007 *Sir Nigel Gresley*, No. 60009 *Union of South Africa* and, of course, the star of the show, No. 4468 *Mallard*.

A full description of these events is contained in our companion publications Mallard 75 and Mallard: The Magnificent Six. Suffice to say, despite doubts expressed by sceptics in earlier stages of the proceedings, Mallard 75 turned out to be one of the most successful events in the history of the railway preservation movement.

Around 364,000 visitors turned up for the three events, and with the help of sponsorship

Princess Coronation Pacific No. 46235 passes Hatch End as works a return football special from Wembley Stadium on May 11, 1963. BARRY AUSTIN

from several key quarters, Mallard 75 turned in a profit of around £500,000 for the Science Museum group.

Not only that, the huge wave of publicity that Mallard 75 generated was credited with turning many non-enthusiast ordinary members of the public on to railway heritage, with the knock-on effect at boosting visitor numbers at preserved lines throughout the country.

Mallard 75 earned the National Railway Museum the Heritage Railway Association's top accolade, the Peter Manisty Award for Excellence 2013.

Inevitably, as the queues to both museums tailed into the distance on virtually every day of the three events, the question was asked in many quarters – how could we follow it up?

The same idea kept cropping up – we've now lined up the LNER A4s, so why not assemble the surviving LMS Pacifics, all of which are in Britain?

CITY OF BIRMINGHAM THE 'LOST' DUCHESS?

It sounds a no brainer, on paper at least. The museum has the restreamlined *Duchess of Hamilton*, while the Princess Royal Class Locomotive Trust owns *Duchess of Sutherland* and *Princess Margaret Rose*. *Princess Elizabeth* would also be readily available.

However, the big problem appears to lie with the third surviving Princess Coronation Pacific, No. 46235, which its Birmingham museum custodians have steadfastly refused to loan out for display or restoration to running order, and it remains the only one of the three survivors never to have steamed in preservation.

Built at Crewe in 1939 to Lot No. 150 as No. 6235, one of the third batch of the class and outshopped on July 31 that year, it was the first Princess Coronation to be fitted with a double chimney as built.

It originally carried a streamlined casing painted in LMS crimson lake, but it was removed in 1946. Indeed, *City of Birmingham* was the first of the class to lose its casing, and in July 1952 it became the first to have its sloping smokebox removed and replaced with a round-topped version.

Like others in the class, it was painted black during the Second World War.

In April 1953, it was fitted with the new smokebox and repainted into the Brunswick green livery which it carries to this day.

This Second World War LMS poster was produced to highlight the continual support that the railway provided to the nation, and showed *City of Birmingham* in its original streamlined form with a replica of Stephenson's *Rocket*. The photograph and lithograph are by J Weiner Ltd of London. NRM

No. 46235 *City of Birmingham* at Acton bridge on the West Coast Main Line in 1962.
BEN BROOKSBANK*

SAVED BY ITS NAME

Birmingham Science Museum approached BR in the Fifties to see if No. 46235 could be obtained for display, once it had been declared redundant, because of its name – the same factor that ensured the survival of the North American A4s.

Historically, No. 46235 had very little to do with Birmingham, apart from being officially named at New Street station on March 20, when a special coat of arms plate was fitted above the nameplate, although it had carried the name since entering traffic. In its working life it rarely ran through the city, as the track through New Street was deemed too tight a curve.

Instead, it was shedded at Crewe North and hauled express passenger trains via the Trent

No. 46235 *City of Birmingham* passes
Hilton Junction with a Perth-Euston
express in June 1963.
P HUGHES/COLOUR RAIL

Valley avoiding section of the West Coast Main Line to Scotland.

No. 46235 covered 1,650,000 miles in service before withdrawal on September 30, 1964.

Considered as the example of the class to be preserved for the nation, British Railways agreed for it to be handed over to the Birmingham museum.

It was prepared by BR at Crewe to full duty specification but never returned to steam, and the view has been expressed that the overhaul was purely cosmetic.

It went into storage at Nuneaton shed during 1965 prior to its arrival in Birmingham in May the following year, when crowds lined city streets to watch it being moved to the Birmingham Museum of Science and Industry situated in Newhall Street.

This museum was housed in the building originally occupied by the Elkington Silver Electroplating Works, which dated from 1838. It was converted into a museum in 1951 and one of its star exhibits was the 1797 Smethwick Engine, built by famous local industrialist James Watt.

I recall being taken to the museum with my brother by our dad in my infant years. Enormously popular with local people, it was packed with what to an infant were weird, wonderful and fascinating objects. Years later, I was delighted to find that another had been added: a giant green steam railway locomotive, which had been displayed in a manner in which the wheels turned fractionally ever hour, via an electric motor which moved the motion. As such, it was a hugely-popular exhibit.

Back in the mid-Sixties, the UK preservation movement was still in its infancy. Indeed, had it been realised that such locomotives would within a decade or so be considered priceless historical artefacts, it is all but certain that homes would have been found for more of the Duchesses that ended up at the scrapyard after being displaced by diesels and electrics. Indeed, if not for Sir Billy Butlin, we would have been left with only one, and that would have surely been a tragedy of epic proportions.

However, as the heritage movement gathered pace, approaches were made to the museum asking if it might be possible to return *City of Birmingham* to steam.

One such approach was made in 1985 by Jon Price, who set up the now defunct

Saturday, September 10, 1966, and No. 46235 *City of Birmingham* waits patiently on its short stretch of track for the new science museum in Newhall Street to house it.
PATRICK O' BRIEN

On December 2, 2000, LMS Princess Coronation Pacific No. 46235 *City of Birmingham* emerged into daylight for the first time in 34 years to be taken by low loader through the city centre after which it is named. The locomotive had remained hidden from view since the museum closed in 2007. To move the 74ft locomotive and tender across the city centre to its new indoor home at the Thinktank museum, as the city centre was teeming with Christmas shoppers, Newhall Street was closed, the wall of the museum had to be demolished and temporary track laid so it could be extracted. The Reverend Tom Pyke, vicar of nearby St Paul's church, was called on to bless No. 46235 at a farewell ceremony. A convoy of vehicles including the Allelys' low loader on which the engine had been loaded followed a route along George Street, Newhall Hill, Summer Row, Paradise Circus, Great Charles Street Queensway, St Chad's Queensway, Lancaster Circus, James Watt Queensway, Jennens Road, Lawley Middleway and Curzon Street, as scores of spectators lined the streets. It was winched into position at Thinktank the next day, the operation being completed two hours ahead of schedule. BIRMINGHAM EVENING MAIL

www.madeinbirmingham.org website, but the curator at the time said that No. 46235 could never be restored because new parts would have to be used and that would be not in line with the policy for the locomotive's preservation at the museum.

MOVE TO THINKTANK

The city council, which owned the popular museum, closed it in 1997, after deciding that repairs to the fabric of the structure would cost too much. The building currently has no permanent use.

After its closure, many of its exhibits were moved across the city centre to Thinktank, a new entrance fee-based exhibition established in a modern oblong gigantic block-like structure in Millennium Point in the regeneration area of Eastside, across the road from the London & Birmingham Railway's classical Curzon Street terminus. The Duchess made the journey by Allelys low loader on December 2, 2000, as crowds again lined the streets.

Millennium Point was a Millennium Commission project, estimated to have cost £114 million, with £50 million provided by the National Lottery. It offered the council the chance to relocate the old museum rather than patch it up.

Described as a multi-use meeting complex, Millennium Point also contains Birmingham School of Acting and Birmingham City University's Faculty of Technology, Engineering and the Environment, part of Birmingham Metropolitan College and a giant screen cinema, as well as Thinktank.

The complex was officially opened by the Queen on July 2, 2002.

Thinktank has four floors of more than 200 hands-on exhibits and artefacts. Each floor has a theme, progressing from the past, in The Past (Level 0), through The Balcony (Level 1) and The Present (Level 2), to the future, in The Future gallery (Level 3).

On the ground floor, behind a huge plate glass window, with access ramps positioned around one side, sits No. 46235.

A sign displayed alongside the locomotive states that it is too tall to run on the modern national network as it would foul overhead electric lines. That is correct, but an overhaul to running order could see the cab and boiler mountings lowered so that it would conform with the modern-day loading gauge, as has been the case with the two other preserved Princess Coronations, the original parts could be refitted when its boiler ticket runs out and it returns to static display.

Over the years, there have been further calls for the museum authorities to allow this magnificent locomotive to be restored to do exactly what it was built for – hauling heavy express passenger trains on the main line – acting as a flagship ambassador for the city in the process.

RESTORATION REBUFFED

And again, each time the museum and city council have flatly refused, giving the same stock curatorial statement, that it is a perfect example of a steam locomotive as overhauled at a BR works, being trotted out, and to run it

No. 46235 *City of Birmingham* on display inside the former Birmingham Museum of Science & Industry in Newhall Street in April 1970. HUGH LLEWELLYN*

A snapshot of *City of Birmingham* being moved into the Newhall Street museum. ROY LAWRANCE

again would destroy this "uniqueness".

When *Heritage Railway* magazine tabled a series of questions to Birmingham Museums about the possibly of releasing No. 46235, if only for a static display LMS line up, PR manageress Clare Fudge: "It is a key feature of the museum and remains a core object within the nationally designated science and industry collections. It has huge importance within the locality and is an example of a British Railways steam locomotive as serviced at a British Railways locomotive works.

"It is fully accessible via a ramp for visitors with mobility impairments and staff are happy to facilitate access to collections items for any enquires. We welcome enquirers who wish to make an appointment with the collections team to view the collections both on display and in store."

Again, its last service at Crewe Works was mentioned. And again, it seems that there is a massive difference between a locomotive being serviced as fit for purpose – that is, another spell of running on the main line – and one that had been withdrawn for the scrapyard but was given what appears to be basically cosmetic spruce-up for permanent static display, if indeed that was the case back in 1965.

The argument used by would-be restorationists is that a basically cosmetic overhaul purely to smarten up an artefact for it to be presented to the public on static display, even if it was carried out by a railway works, has little heritage merit in itself.

The question was asked – would the museum consider loaning No. 46235 (a) on static display, to a venue like the National Railway Museum in York, maybe on short-term loan, or (b), to a

The Duchess inside the Newhall Street museum in 1978. BARRY LEWIS*

proven body like Tyseley Locomotive Works for overhaul to running order?

The answer came thus: "It has huge importance within the locality and would be sorely missed by visitors should it not be on display within Birmingham.

"It represents the best of Birmingham's railway heritage and the museum sees its role as conserving the engine for as long as possible by limiting the exposure to agents of

deterioration for future generations to enjoy.

"We are sympathetic to those that would wish to see it steam but have to walk a fine line but preservation in perpetuity and access.

"It is not feasible to loan this item to other museums as it would cost thousands of pounds to undertake the work needed to do this (safe disassembly and removal, disruption to fabric of museum building and galleries, reassembly etc).

"Museums abide by strict ethical guidelines.

A pinnacle of railway heritage: the National Railway Museum's Mallard 75 celebrations will be remembered for decades to come, if only for this iconic image from the evening photographic charter at the Great Goodbye. It was the last of three Great Gatherings of all six surviving Gresley A4 streamlined Pacifics, held at the Locomotion museum in Shildon from February 15-23. From left to right on February 19 are postwar steam record holder No. 60007 *Sir Nigel Gresley*, No. 60008 *Dwight D. Eisenhower,* No. 60009 *Union of South Africa,* No. 4489 *Dominion of Canada*; heritage era steam record holder No. 4464 *Bittern* and world steam railway speed record holder No. 4468 *Mallard.* Princess coronation 4-6-2 No. 46235 *City of Birmingham* is the missing piece of the jigsaw that would allow a similar line up of all five surviving LMS Pacifics. FRED KERR

A scale model of *City of Birmingham* in its LMS streamlined days is displayed inside Thinktank. ROBIN JONES

On December 3, 2000, *City of Birmingham* stands inside the Thinktank museum, before a giant plate glass window was installed, sealing it inside. BIRMINGHAM EVENING MAIL

To safeguard this item we would only loan this item to an accredited museum.

"No accredited museums have to date expressed an interest in requesting the loan of this item. It is highly unlikely that in these harsh economic times any accredited museums would be able to justify the expense associated with this loan.

"As the best-preserved engine of this class it contains the most original parts of any example of its significance is therefore deemed too great to put at risk of deterioration by steaming. Instead it acts as a benchmark and reference point to the others of its class that are in steam."

PROMPTING MORE QUESTIONS

Again, this answer raises many more questions, especially in view of the success of Mallard 75.

What exactly, is the level of the "huge importance" of No. 46235, within the locality, apart from its name from the fact it has been displayed in a museum there for around half a century? Might No. 46235 have infinitely greater importance to Birmingham if it acted as a living, steaming, roving advertisement for this city with its colossal proud manufacturing heritage, and an artefact that would, like the line-up of six A4s, grab the imagination of the city's future generations?

Would *City of Birmingham* be sorely missed by visitors if it was temporarily displayed at a location outside Thinktank, maybe just for a few weeks? Would city residents throw up their hands in horror if they saw No. 46235 steaming on the main line rather than penned into its slot on the ground floor of Thinktank?

Surely if the Duchess was removed from the museum for a loan spell, another railway locomotive could immediately take its place in the berth, one of equal magnitude – *Mallard* maybe – which might encourage repeat visitors to Thinktank while it was there?

Furthermore, how on earth does a Duchess represent the "best of Birmingham's railway heritage"?

Firstly, the class was not built anywhere near Birmingham, and secondly, it was only in the last few years of BR steam when their days were numbered and being ousted from premier duties by modern traction that the class was used on West Coast Main Line services into New Street, instead taking the Trent Valley Line avoiding route.

Again, it boils down to the fact that like *Dwight D. Eisenhower* and *Dominion of Canada*, No. 46235's only cast-iron connection with its permanent home is its name.

Surely if a replacement exhibit of similar stature and public appeal was found during a loan spell, it might far better represent Birmingham's railway heritage – maybe a GWR King or Castle, world-beating classes regularly seen at Snow Hill station, or another LMS type that regularly passed through New Street.

By contrast, a pure Birmingham thoroughbred locomotive is Secundus, which in 2004 was placed on long-term loaned by none other than Birmingham Museums to the Purbeck Mineral and Mining Museum next to the Swanage Railway's Norden park-and-ride station in deepest Dorset.

Built in Birmingham by Bellis & Seekings Ltd in 1874 for the 2ft 8½in gauge Furzebrook Railway, this unique 0-6-0WT worked in Purbeck until 1955 and was saved by the Birmingham Locomotive Club which persuaded the scrap company to donate it for preservation.

Surrounded by public access ramps inside the Thinktank museum, No. 46235 *City of Birmingham* is somewhat difficult to photograph. ROBIN JONES

Its initial loan to the Purbeck group, for static display only, was arranged by none other than Birmingham Museums' head of curatorial services Jane Arthur. If such a Birmingham born and bred locomotive can be loaned out for several years, why not a Crewe-built one for a few weeks?

A Great Gathering line-up of LMS Pacifics would not need *City of Birmingham* to be overhauled either to running order or even cosmetically. It would stay exactly in the condition that it is now in. All that would be needed would be for it to be carried under protective sheeting on the back of a low loader.

Also, Thinktank could insist that its temporary loan display would be under cover, thereby removing any fears that its paintwork would be damaged by the elements.

As for the thousands of pounds that it would cost to remove No. 46235 from Thinktank, this would be a tiny drop in the ocean compared to the expense and immense difficulty involved in the repatriation of the North American A4s. In the case of Thinktank, one large plate glass window would need to be removed.

Two thirds of the cost of the repatriation of the A4s was covered by outside sponsorship. I'm absolutely sure that someone, somewhere, would cover the meagre amount by comparison that it would cost to extract and replace *City of Birmingham* inside Thinktank. And again, look at those Mallard 75 visitor numbers – and then seriously tell me that the costs could not be covered. Many times over.

The National Railway Museum is an accredited museum. If it decided to follow

City of Birmingham displayed inside Thinktank. The engine is separated from the tender with a walkway installed inbetween, for visitors to inspect the cab. ROBIN JONES

up its Mallard 75 plateau with a similar event honouring the derring-do records set by the LMS and its locomotive crews in the Thirties, after reaping the rewards from the Great Gathering in "these harsh economic times", it might just be persuaded to go for spending what is surely a trifling amount with massive rewards.

The potential need to replace original parts is regularly given by museums as a reason for not returning a particular locomotive to steam.

Again, the worn original parts that have to be replaced need not be discarded but could be preserved, maybe on display, or perhaps in a museum store, for scrutiny on request. Nothing needs to be destroyed nor thrown away, and if it was deemed absolutely necessary for some reason, they could be refitted at a future date.

Also, it is likely, indeed almost certain, that many of the components of No. 46235 are by no means original to the locomotive in question, but had been carried by sisters, and

The Thinktank museum is housed in Millennium Point near the former Curzon Street station. Critics have said that the modern museum lacks the ambience of its much-loved predecessor in **Newhall Street.** ROBIN JONES

City of Birmingham stands just yards away from a plate glass window which, if lifted out, would allow the Duchess to be extracted to visit other venues if permission was ever given. ROBIN JONES

exchanged during overhauls. Replacing parts is not necessarily damaging heritage, but merely continuing the history of a locomotive in the way that designers intended.

Of course, there are examples of rolling stock where restoration would all but destroy every piece of surviving original fabric, like the Stephenson's *Rocket* in the Science Museum, or the original *Puffing Billy*, and could never be justified under any circumstances.

Such cases apart, I maintain that the best way to showcase a locomotive is to use it for the purpose for which it came into existence in the first place – to haul trains.

As it is, the position of No. 46235 inside Thinktank has attracted criticism that it is cramped and difficult to see and photograph, unlike the exhibits in the National Railway Museum and other heritage railway venues.

Indeed, Thinktank has had more than its

fair share of critics. When it opened, traditionalists slated it for its very modern design as compared to the historic Newhall Street building, which they felt had more empathy with the artefacts displayed there.

A FUTURE WIN-WIN SITUATION?

The legal owner of No. 46235 and the other exhibits inside Thinktank is Birmingham City Council.

Keith Whitmore, a director of the Bahamas Locomotive Society who is also chairman of the Heaton Park Tramway Trust on behalf of the Manchester City Council, wrote to Birmingham City Council leader Albert Bore, and said: "Many including myself feel that the loco could be much better used as a roving ambassador for the city rather than shoved into a corner so poorly displayed."

An honorary alderman of Manchester City Council, a director of the Royal Exchange Theatre in Manchester, and a director of the People's History Museum, Keith added: "If the loco were overhauled at Tyseley to main line running, then everywhere it went Birmingham's name would be seen positively and could be used to promote the city."

Steve Davies, the originator of Mallard 75, said: "We have already seen how such events represent a win-win situation for all concerned. So what could come next?

"The obvious answer is to gather all five surviving LMS pacifics. Yes, I know that *City of Birmingham* is hermetically sealed into its Thinktank Birmingham Science Museum display building.

Classic GWR motive power around the turntable at Tyseley Locomotive Works in Birmingham on June 26, 2009: from left to right are 4-6-0s No. 4936 *Kinlet Hall*, No. 7029 *Clun Castle*, No. 4953 *Pitchford Hall* and pannier No. 9600. Surely this would make an ideal venue for a future line up of all five surviving LMS Pacifics, and if a decision was ever made to allow No. 46235 *City of Birmingham* to be restored to running order, the site boasts one of the finest modern steam engineering workshops. ROBIN JONES

"But surely the temporary release of the locomotive from its current location would represent a very minor challenge compared with the gathering of all the A4s and would of course be a public spectacle and marketing tool in its own right.

"We have seen how the release and movement of *Dominion of Canada* and *Dwight D. Eisenhower* became an event of international interest and significance and set the marketing conditions which helped Mallard 75 become the runaway success it has turned out to be.

"As a result, the two respective owning museums, Exporail – The Canadian Railway Museum, Montreal, and the National Railroad Museum, Green Bay, Wisconsin are enjoying unprecedented levels of international awareness and brand recognition.

"The extraction and movement of *City of Birmingham* would be no different in its overall beneficial impact on public awareness of Thinktank, and would, I forecast, help to maintain the huge momentum of enthusiast and non-enthusiast support for railways, and railway heritage in particular, which Mallard 75 has achieved. Railway history is fashionable again. Let's keep it that way."

COULD NO. 46235 BE SOLD?

The city council was again asked in late 2013 if, in view of budget cutbacks in services, No. 46235 could be sold off to help pay the Birmingham City Council's debts, a written reply which came via Janet Priestley, head of press, PR and communications, said: "The pressures that we face in Birmingham are of such a magnitude, that all options are being explored at the moment, and we are currently in the middle of a public discussion about what how we do things differently in the future."

However, a subsequent statement from the press office, said: "Returning the locomotive to working order is not an issue that BCC is currently considering.

"BCC has not changed its policy to preserve the engine in the condition that it left service. The locomotive is viewed and enjoyed by the 200,000 people in its present location, and remains a popular exhibit with all visitors to Thinktank.

"The locomotive is being well cared for. It will survive in its present environment for generations and it may be that those future generations take a decision to restore the locomotive or perhaps they will be grateful that it has been preserved in its 'as used' condition and will act as a rich research resource for scholars and enthusiasts in the future."

Tyseley Locomotive Works Bob Meanley, praised for his restreamlining of No. 6229 *Duchess of Hamilton* said he would be happy to restore No. 46235 if asked, but pointed there is a ticking time bomb in the form of the locomotive's blue asbestos content.

Under current legislation, it is likely that one day it will need removing, potentially leaving the cash-pressed council with a large bill, unless a sponsor found. Such work would eradicate the engine's perceived status as being in the exact condition that it left BR in.

Nevertheless, the locomotive is safe, and under cover. The North American museums said that their A4s would never returned to

The coat of arms of the city of Birmingham is displayed above the nameplates. ROBIN JONES

An oblique view of No. 46235 inside Thinktank. ROBIN JONES

Britain, but Steve Davies found a way through the minefield to make it happen. Railway preservation has time and time again proved that it is the art of the possible, and so while No. 46235 exists and is complete, a possibility, no matter how slim, will always exist.

If the controversial HS2 link to London is built, Birmingham's terminus will be the old Curzon Street station. Behind its plate glass window, No. 46235 will be within striking distance of the 225mph trains arriving and departing.

Will they be as big an inspiration to future generations as the Duchesses were to theirs? ∎

On May 17, 2013, prior to the Mallard 75 series of events, the newly-varnished cosmetically-overhauled temporarily repatriated A4 No. 4489 *Dominion of Canada* was hauled out of the Locomotion museum at Shildon and lined up alongside one-time rival *Duchess of Hamilton.* ANTHONY COULLS

SQUARING UP TO THE OPPOSITION

One of the biggest riddles in British railway history remains to be answered, and never will be.

Could a Princess Coronation Pacific have taken the world steam speed record off *Mallard*?

Answering the question comes straight up against a basic hurdle from the start – what is a world speed record?

In the field of athletics, it is simple. An athlete performs a feat across a measured distance, a uniform standard accepted the world over.

However, I much prefer the field of football as a comparison with the railway sector.

Take a football league in which every team's home pitch is a different size, never mind the slope. Of course, if every team has to play at every ground at least once, then the discrepancies should, in theory, even themselves out somewhat. Yet if old Yeovil Town or the 3G pitch side find themselves

leading the pack, inevitably rival fans will say it is because they have an unfair home advantage because they are acclimatised to playing on it every week.

In railways, there has never been a universal standard for speed records, apart from the official endorsement of speed runs recorded on specialist instrumentation. Yes, GWR 4-4-0 No. 3440 *City of Truro* probably did exceed 100mph on Wellington Bank in 1904, but the accuracy of timers holding stopwatches is never going to match up to the data recorded by experts in a dynamometer car. And how do you compare Wellington Bank with Madeley Bank, where No. 6220 *Coronation* hit either 113mph or 114mph, or Stoke Bank, scene of *Mallard's* achievement on July 3, 1938?

Coronation's record run began on Madeley Bank, which is 1¾ miles at 1-in-177 followed by 2¾ miles at 1-in-69. Stoke Bank has a gradient of three miles at 1-in-178, 1½ miles at 1-in-330

or level, and 4½ miles at 1-in-200, and lasts for the best part of 20 miles from Stoke summit running almost to Peterborough itself.

Apart from being downward slopes, none of these gradients can therefore be said to be alike.

Then there comes into play the load that a particular locomotive was hauling. *Coronation* had eight coaches behind it – a gross load of 270 tons behind the tender – when Tom Clark caused the crockery to break, while *Mallard's* train was seven coaches long, comprising a load of 240 tons, over what may be regarded as a more favourable gradient.

Unlike world records for cars and aircraft, there is no requirement to take an average of two runs in both directions, and assistance from the gradient or wind has always been acceptable in rail speed records.

When the German Class 05 three-cylinder 4-6-4 took the world speed record in 1936 with a speed of 124.5mph, it was hauling only four coaches, a load of 197 tons. Yet the section of

Marking the 75th birthday of *Duchess of Hamilton*, in September 2013 at the Locomotion museum, the locomotive was reunited with the bell which it carried of its tour of the US as No. 6220 *Coronation* in 1939. ADRIAN SCALES/229 CLUB

the Berlin to Hamburg line on which the speed was achieved is flat.

It is therefore logical to assume that had exactly the same locomotive and train had the benefit of the Stoke Bank gradient, it would have beaten *Mallard's* record with a heavier loading. Maybe its middle big end may not have overheated in the process: *Mallard* had to be taken off the train at Peterborough and sent back to Doncaster for repairs. By contrast, the Borsig 05 suffered no damage during its record run.

To this day, many German specialists maintain that the record attained by No. 05.002, during which it was recorded as having produced more than 3400 indicated (as opposed to drawbar) horsepower, is in essence superior to that set by *Mallard*.

A counter argument here is that while Gresley with *Mallard* and indeed Stanier with No. 6220 staged just one attempt at the record, the Germans had made several 'practice' runs beforehand, on complete journeys between Hamburg and Berlin. On June 7, 1935, No. 05.002 hit 119.1mph, and went on the make six more runs over 110mph) with trains up to 250 tons.

By contrast, despite the advantage of the slope, the circumstances of *Mallard's* run were far from perfect, with a 15mph permanent way check north of Grantham. Again, the 'level playing field' concept is invoked, from yet another perspective.

'If' is the magic word here. Maybe, if not probably, the German locomotive could have topped 126mph with *Mallard's* train. There again, if *Mallard* driver Joe Duddington had not been told to ease off before Essendine

Tunnel and the curves beyond were reached, could he have reached 130mph or maybe more? He and his traction inspector certainly believed he could have done, and publicly said so immediately afterwards.

Gresley too believed that an A4 could reach 130mph, and indeed planned to have another attempt on the record in September 1939, but was prevented by the outbreak of the Second World War.

There is an unconfirmed story from the Fifties that on arrival at King's Cross with a late-running Up express, the driver and fireman of A4 No. 60017 *Silver Fox* were immediately suspended for two weeks for having been clocked at 130mph – on where else but Stoke Bank.

During the Mallard 75 celebrations, a gathering of former A4 drivers took place at the National Railway Museum in York. There were anecdotal talks of 130mph having been passed, and one story bandied about was that of 140mph having been seen on a footplate speedometer by one of the drivers in attendance, but without any form of verification whatsoever.

In the US, the Pennsylvania Railroad's S1 prototype was unofficially clocked at 127mph, and the Chicago, Milwaukee, St Paul & Pacific Railroad streamlined Class F7 4-6-4 was another claimed to have exceeded 126mph.

In August 1940, French expert Baron Gérard Vuillet logged a report of a Milwaukee Road Chicago to St Paul Hiawatha repeatedly

exceeding 125mph through Wisconsin. His report noted that the US crews did not consider their speed remarkable, but was merely what they had to do to maintain the schedule. Again, no official records exist to confirm such accounts.

In the case of No. 6220 *Coronation*, the three official records on board agreed to the probability of a slight peak of 113mph, thereby equalling, but not in itself bettering, the LNER record set in August 1936. This was by No. 2512 *Silver Fox* heading the 'Silver Jubilee' down Stoke Bank, although, as we have seen, the LMS claimed a new 114mph UK record indicated by another instrument.

Sadly, the LMS did not have a Stoke Bank equivalent, and it is highly unlikely that the LNER board let alone Gresley would have agreed to a comparative test between a Duchess and an A4 on its Lincolnshire racetrack to settle the issue.

While the three-cylinder A4s were built for speed, and have a tractive effort of 35,455lb-ft, the four-cylinder Princess Coronation Pacifics have a tractive effort of 40,000lb-ft, essential for hauling 16 or 17-coach trains over Shap or Beattock.

ABSOLUTE POWER

In respect of tractive effort alone, the Princess Coronation Pacifics cannot be described as the most powerful British locomotive. That honour goes to the six Gresley P2 2-8-2s, built for the gruelling Edinburgh to Aberdeen route, and

Duchess of Hamilton and Dominion of Canada 'on shed' inside Locomotion in May 2013.
LOCOMOTION

which had a tractive effort of 43,462lb-ft, making them in this respect the most powerful express passenger locomotive to ever run in Britain. A seventh example, No. 2007 *Prince of Wales*, is currently being built by The A1 Steam Locomotive Trust, builder and operator of new-build A1 Peppercorn Pacific No. 60163 *Tornado*.

However, tractive effort does not equal speed: the P2s had smaller wheels that A4s or Duchesses, and the fastest speed recorded by one of them was 82.5mph on test on the main line in France, so they are ruled out of this debate.

The Duchesses had a remarkable power output for their size when compared to bigger locomotives, both at home and abroad. As we have seen, in 1939, No. 6234 *Duchess of Abercorn* achieved 3300 horsepower while hauling a test train up to Beattock summit. This figure for absolute power has never been bettered by a British steam locomotive.

For comparison, A4 No. 4901 *Capercaillie* in 1940 exerted 2200 drawbar horsepower on the straight and level track north of York when hauling 21 coaches (730 tons gross) at an average of 75.9 mph for 25 miles.

The highest recorded power output from an A4 was 2450 drawbar horsepower

when *Mallard* hauled 11 coaches (415 tons gross) up Stoke Bank at a sustained 80mph in 1963. The writer O S Nock considered this performance to be superior to *Mallard's* world record feat in 1938.

By comparison, the highest possible drawbar horsepower from a Class 40 diesel, a class designed to replace the A4s and Duchesses, was 1450, although it could be achieved over long distances and without effort from the crew.

My feeling is that the absolute power of a Princess Coronation Pacific may well, indeed would probably, have triumphed over an A4 on a like-for-like racetrack and with an identical loading. Had circumstances been different, a Duchess might one day have taken the world record.

Despite the speed that *Mallard* achieved in 1938, it was not generating as much horsepower in so doing as a Duchess climbing Shap and Beattock at more than 50mph with 600-plus tons of heavy sleeping cars in tow in the middle of the night.

Even before the war, a Stanier Duchess had produced more horsepower in its cylinders than even the Class 55 Deltics could achieve a generation later. Yet had it not been for the Second World War, the Duchesses in all

probability would have been surpassed, by another Stanier masterpiece.

Before war broke out, Stanier was considering a four-cylinder compound 4-6-4 which would comprise essentially a Duchess boiler combined with a larger firebox that would be so big as to require a four-wheel trailing truck to carry it.

There would have been a 70ft gate area, mechanical stoker firing and numerous other refinements based mainly on the work of Andre Chapelon in France.

The schematic drawings are all held in the archives at the National Railway Museum in York. Maybe one day, somebody might launch a project to build what might have been British steam's greatest might-have-been had the world not been overtaken by events.

There again, had the Second World War not intervened, Britain would most likely have followed the same course as the US and introduced modern traction much earlier than it did, with a permanent half called to any further steam locomotive designs.

Speaking after the demise of the Duchesses in 1964, railway photographer the late Derek Cross said: "After the trout had quit the pond, only the minnows remained."

He would have been aware that A4s, BR Standard Britannia 4-6-2s and Bulleid Pacifics would still have been running.

Duchess of Hamilton and *Dominion of Canada* side by side inside the Locomotion exhibition hall at Shildon. ANTHONY COULLS

Great rivals from the Thirties united outside the National Railway Museum on May 22, 2009: No. 6229 *Duchess of Hamilton* and visiting LNER A4 Pacific No. 60009 *Union of South Africa*. PHILIP BENHAM

Two Stanier crimson lake classics reunited: Jubilee 4-6-0 No. 45699 *Galatea* and *Duchess of Hamilton* at Locomotion on September 20, 2013, at the start of an LMS-themed weekend held to mark the 75th birthday of No. 6229. NRM

THANKS TO THE B TEAM!

If only had the Duchesses lasted in service another two or three years longer, more examples of one of the finest forms of transport technology anywhere in the world almost certainly survive today.

As it was, most of them went on one-way trips to the scrapyard within months of withdrawal. Only Woodham Brothers scrapyard in Barry had a policy of not cutting locomotives up immediately, and the nascent preservation movement therefore had a decade or two in which to grow to the point where large numbers could be bought for heritage movement. Barry bought scrap locomotives mainly from the Southern and Western regions, and so other areas lost out. Yes, we have three Duchesses today, but 30 Bulleid Pacifics, several of which are yet to resteam.

In the summer 1968, the late Morecambe GP and preservation powerhouse Dr Peter Beet spent a few frantic weeks of the dying days of British Rail main line steam haulage with friends saving several Stanier 'Black Fives'. If only the Duchesses could have lingered on until then.

As it is, we have the 'B team' to thank for the survival of the trio. First and foremost comes Billy Butlin, without whom the real US tour star *Duchess of Hamilton* and *Duchess of Sutherland* would have long ago been turned into razor blades. Then there is Birmingham City Council, which gave a ready home for the

class member named after the city, even though its other historic links with Birmingham remain questionable. Why on earth did other museums in cities like Leeds, Liverpool, Manchester, Sheffield and Chester, not follow suit, and take locomotives carrying 'their' nameplates?

Next in the B list comes Alan Bloom, whose Bressingham Steam Museum provided a superb safe haven for several steam locomotives in the great uncertainty of the Sixties.

Then there is Bob Meanley at Tyseley Locomotive Works, who did such an amazing job on now only recreating the streamlined casing of *Duchess of Hamilton* on behalf of the Friends of the National Railway Museum, but adapted it to fit the modern network loading gauge, in readiness for the eagerly-awaited day when it returns to steams.

Finally, special thanks must go to Brell Ewart, who as chairman of the Princess Royal Class Locomotive Trust, negotiated both the release of *Duchess of Sutherland* and sizeable Heritage Lottery Fund grant aid to restore No. 6233 to steam on the main line, as a defining preservation icon. Thanks to Brell, the last of the B team, we all have the pleasure of seeing, photographing and riding behind a Duchess today.

Today we have several truly magnificent steam locomotives running over the national network, but as a personal favourite, one of

them just about nudges it every time for me, whether it is painted maroon, black or green.

While Birmingham richly deserves 11 out of 10 for saving No. 6235 and giving it half a century of safe undercover accommodation, my personal view is that it is a national treasure that is wasted where it is.

I have never been happy with the cramped way in which it is displayed in the Thinktank museum, which for me has far less appeal than its quite marvellous Birmingham Museum of Science and Industry box of delights predecessor. Thinktank stands opposite the London & Birmingham Railway's original Curzon Street terminus, which is due to be given a new lease of life if and when the High Speed 2 project gives the second city and superfast link to the capital.

If No. 6235 must remain as a static exhibit, what better place to display it for maximum impact than inside the new HS2 terminal, as a monument to the days when British transport technology, in particular the creations of Stanier and Gresley, led the world?

For me, however, the best way to preserve a steam locomotive is by having it do the job it was built to do – hauling trains.

And what better an advertisement for the city of Birmingham today than, when HS2 is complete, having No. 6235 restored by the experts down the road at Tyseley three miles away, and then hauling the ceremonial first train over the new route? ∎